COMBAT AIRCRAFT SERIES

MiG-23/-27
Flogger

BILL GUNSTON

OSPREY PUBLISHING LONDON

Published in 1986 by
Osprey Publishing Ltd
Member Company of the George Philip Group
12–14 Long Acre, London WC2E 9LP

British Library Cataloguing in Publication Data

Gunston, Bill
  MiG-23/27 Flogger.–(Osprey combat aircraft)
  1. MIG (Fighter planes)
  I. Title
  623.74'63 UG1242.F5

ISBN 0-85045-718-1

Typeset by Flair plan Photo-typesetting Ltd.
Printed by Proost International Book Production,
Turnhout, Belgium.

Colour artworks: pages 30-31 (except bottom), and
page 32, © Pilot Press Ltd.; remainder © Bedford
Editions (jacket, pages 26-27 Mike Keep).
Cutaway drawing: © Pilot Press Ltd.
Diagrams: Seb Quigley.
Photographs: pages 28 and 30, © Lennart Berns,
Aeroproduction; remainder supplied by Pilot Press
Ltd., and the United States Department of Defense, all
of whom the publishers would like to thank.

The Author

BILL GUNSTON, former RAF pilot and flying
instructor, is an internationally acknowledged expert on
aircraft and aviation affairs. He is the author of
numerous books on the subject, is a frequent
broadcaster, was technical editor of "Flight
International" and technology editor of "Science
Journal", and is assistant compiler of "Jane's All The
World's Aircraft".

Contents

1
Background

FOR ABOUT 15 years the MiG-23 family, in its various versions, has been manufactured in larger numbers than any contemporary combat aircraft (if one excludes the Mi-8 helicopter, whose output over the same period nears 10,000). On this count alone it must rate as one of the most important warplanes of today's world, and it is also a design of uncommon technical interest. To make it harder, however, it is not one type of aircraft but several, though all share the same basic airframe structure.

Some are dedicated night and adverse-weather interceptors, able to kill other aircraft at a distance but with limited close air combat capability and even fewer pretensions at flying attack missions. Most of the rest are dedicated ground-attack aircraft, extremely formidable under many conditions but lacking some of the avionic items needed for penetration at the lowest level and accurate delivery of weapons in bad weather, and with only the most limited

air-combat capability. The remainder are dual-control trainers.

This is an impressive list, and the fact that there are three distinct versions cannot be taken as criticism, or suggesting lack of versatility in the basic aircraft. There are the same three versions of Tornado, and had the customers asked for it both the Tornado and the MiG-23 could have been delivered as an all-can-do multirole aircraft able to fly fighter, attack and training missions. The difference would be that it would not have been so good at any of them as is today's tailor-made aircraft. Continuing with analysis of missions, it is perhaps surprising that, by mid-1986 at least, no versions of MiG-23 had appeared dedicated to either reconnaissance or electronic warfare. It so happens that a further batch of Tornadoes does include an ECR (electronic combat

Below: The MiG-23MF version known to NATO as Flogger-G is better known in the West than any other variant. This photograph was taken in France in 1978.

and reconnaissance) version, but this is neither a normal "reconnaissance" platform nor an ECM jammer. The MiG-23 would be an outstanding aircraft in either role.

To understand the MiG-23 family it is necessary first to have a broad idea of how the Soviet aircraft industry is organized. There are no "manufacturers" in the sense understood in the West. Requirements for new aircraft are issued from time to time by the VVS (air force), AV-MF (naval aviation), PVO (air defence organization) or GVF (civil air fleet). If a requirement cannot be met by an existing or derivative aircraft then, if it is sufficiently important, a contract is placed with at least one OKB (experimental construction bureau) for a design to meet the requirement. If possible awards will be made to two OKBs, because head-on competition is valued very highly. If possible the new design will use existing engines, radar and other equipment; if not, new designs for these too will be placed under contract with the KBs specializing in such items.

Research institutes

The design teams do not work by themselves. The aircraft team have to discuss their proposals not only with the customer but also with many of the scientific/technical research institutes, of which the most important is TsAGI, the central aerodynamics and hydrodynamics institute. TsAGI is extremely large and powerful, and its aerodynamicists like to be several years head of the design teams at the OKBs. In the case of supersonic fighter and attack aircraft TsAGI can almost dictate the shape that will be adopted. Thus, during the Korean War period (1950-53) TsAGI came up with two wings with leading-edge sweep of 57° for future Mach 2 fighters, one a delta and the other a slender swept wing, in both cases matched with a horizontal tail. Both the MiG (Mikoyan/Guryevich) and Su (Sukhoi) OKBs built prototypes of both configurations, the smaller of the deltas going into production as the MiG-21 and the larger of both the delta and swept-wing aircraft going into production as the Su-9 and Su-7 respectively.

Within the OKBs each new design and prototype has its own designation. It is only when the decision has been taken to build in quantity that a service designation (such as those just given) is alotted; previously the MiG-21 was the Ye-6 and 6B, the Su-7 the S-22 and the Su-9 the T-40. Once accepted, the new type is assigned to one of the dozens of giant GAZ (state aviation factory) complexes which today cover the whole vast extent of the Soviet Union (before 1941 every GAZ was in Russia, and vulnerable to the German invasion). Most GAZ tend to specialize; two of them have built MiG combat aircraft for 40 years, but always know that their next type might be designed by a different OKB. Of course the OKBs always build their own prototypes and development aircraft.

Presented with a similar set of circumstances, a design team in one country may well come up with answers very much like a design team in another.

Below: The Original Ye-231 prototype, precursor of the Flogger series, was publicly demonstrated—and very convincingly—at the Aviation Day display at a Moscow airport on 9 July 1967. It had a different engine from today's MiG-23s, and the wings were mounted further to the rear.

Above: The chief inspiration for the Ye-231 programme was unquestionably the USAF's TFX (later F-111) programme, which found its first production application in the F-111A as seen here.

Despite this, the objective observer would certainly think that, since the late 1950s, the Soviet designers (or rather the TsAGI management) have become almost mesmerized by the new combat aircraft produced in the USA, and especially those built for the USAF. Nowhere is this influence more evident than in the first generation of swing-wing (variable-sweep) aircraft designed in the Soviet Union, one of which launched the aircraft described in this book. Variable-sweep wings had been studied by the Germans in World War 2, the Messerschmitt P.1101 being the basis of the American Bell X-5 flown in 1951. It is thus hardly a new idea, but the early attempts at building a VG (variable-geometry) aircraft were flawed by clumsy design and the belief that the wing roots had to slide axially to front and rear in order to keep the centre of lift approximately in line with the centre of gravity.

Swing-wing advantages

The advantages of variable sweep are fairly obvious, in that the best wing for slow speeds is not the best wing for high speeds. The modern attack aircraft needs to penetrate hostile airspace as low as possible, in dense air, at the highest possible speed. This demands the smallest wing possible, and in particular the shortest possible wingspan, both to reach the necessary speed and to ride through turbulent air in comfort. The wing loading (weight supported by each square foot or square metre) has to be as high as possible. But at takeoff or landing the ideal attack wing would cease to support the aircraft at any speed below about 350 knots! To enable the heavy aircraft to use ordinary airstrips, and to loiter at low speeds, it needs the longest, slenderest, widest-span wings possible, liberally endowed with powerful slats and flaps to give enormously greater lift at low speeds.

Fixed-geometry aircraft have to be an imperfect compromise. The MiG-21, for example, takes off and lands fast, and cannot carry heavy loads. One way of trying to overcome the problem is to add special lift jets, which at takeoff bear perhaps half the weight of the laden aircraft. The lightly loaded wing can then lift the aircraft off at a relatively low speed. The MiG OKB investigated this arrangement with a modified MiG-21, and also built a completely new aircraft which combined a large delta wing—similar to one previously used on large interceptor prototypes—with a modified fuselage and tail from the Ye-230 series, which were the prototypes of the MiG-23. After evaluating the jet-lift demonstrator, which had the figure 23 painted on it but is believed to have been the Ye-230, the unanimous decision was taken to go for swing wings instead. These were tested, alongside the jet-lift aircraft, in the Ye-231.

When these aircraft were being designed, in 1960–65, it was expected that the USAF and US Navy would both buy large numbers of swing-wing F-111s, together with all NATO allies and foreign customers. The F-111's problems were unexpected, and most had little to do with what the MiG OKB saw as shortcomings in the US aircraft. Among these were side-by-side seats, very short engine inlet ducts, inability to use body-mounted pylons (except for a small pylon at the rear for an ECM jammer) and excessive size and weight. Thus, though the F-111 provided a basic technical underpinning in this totally new swing-wing configuration, the MiG designers departed from it in several major respects—and never regretted doing so.

2
Design and Development

I N FACT it was not the Americans that solved the problem of how to design a swing-wing aircraft but the British. Vickers-Armstrongs at Weybridge perfected the basic geometry of the VG wing pivoted well out from the fuselage on a fixed "glove" (triangular inner wing) in 1958. Just at this time the British Government decided, in its wisdom, that there was never going to be any future need for fighters or bombers, and the whole programme was handed to the newly formed NASA in the USA. From that moment, NASA worked on VG wings at Langley Research Center, and it all came together in perfect time for the TFX project, which became the F-111.

Soviets avoid US mistakes

This seemed to the Russians to be the right way to go, and as with the previous generation it was decided that the MiG OKB would design a modest fighter-size machine, while Sukhoi would use exactly the same shape in a larger long-range attack and inter-diction aircraft. The latter, which became the Su-24 (NATO name Fencer), is a very close parallel to the F-111, but the Soviets wisely did not try to pretend it was a fighter, and thus they avoided some design and political problems that almost crippled the F-111.

Thanks to the engine KBs of A. M. Lyul'ka and S. K. Tumanskii, afterburning turbojets were available more powerful than any developed in other countries, and this made it possible for the MiG Ye-23 family to be single-engined. This was despite the fact that, by adopting the VG layout, they could weigh more than twice as much as the previous-generation MiG-21. Of course, had the weight been kept down by making the new machine a short-range day fighter like the MiG-21 then, with the formidable engine and swing wing, the result would have been a dramatic performer indeed. It would have been able to use airstrips 300m (1,000ft) long or less, thereafter climbing vertically and flying rings round every other aircraft in the sky. It would certainly have outper-formed the early lightweight F-16s, besides having far better STOL capability.

This would have been exciting, but at that time close air combat was out of fashion and it was not what the customer wanted. Instead, the tremendous boost in lifting capability was made to lift a much heavier aircraft. Compared with a MiG-21F the new Ye-23 family had twice the wing lift (from a wing only 17 per cent larger in area), twice the engine thrust, twice the internal fuel capacity and more than twice the gross weight. This naturally opened up vastly expanded mission capabilities. In the intercep-tor role the new aircraft could carry a much bigger and more capable radar and a considerably heavier load of missiles and tanks. Thus it could detect and lock-on to enemy aircraft from a distance increased from 12.5 to 53 miles (20 to 85km), with a fair degree of the newly demanded "look down, shoot down" capability against aircraft flying only just above the ground, fire missiles from a distance of up to 22 miles (35km), and, with wings spread out to full span, loiter at low speeds for six hours—all far beyond the capability of the MiG-21.

Fighter and attack versions

In the attack mission it would be possible to carry several times the weapon load of a MiG-21—for example, 16 FAB-250 bombs each weighing 550lb (250kg)—along with a more comprehensive kit of EW self-defence systems, and fly much further to a target. There the weapons could be delivered with higher accuracy, using new avionics not present in the MiG-21, with survivability further enhanced by the ability to fly closer to the ground at much higher speed without unacceptable pilot discomfort, and also by much greater armour protection not present in the MiG-21. But the decision had to be faced: the choice was to build a compromised all-can-do aircraft, or build two quite different versions of the same basic design, incapable of conversion from one to the other. The latter course was adopted, so that there are MiG-23 fighters and MiG-23 (or MiG-27) attackers. All have the same NATO name of Flogger, distinguished by suffix letters.

High-mounted wings

Taking their cue from the American TFX, TsAGI agreed that swing wings are best mounted high on the fuselage, where the massive carry-through box linking the left and right pivots can be placed above the engine ducts and tankage. This also gives enhanced lift over the top of the wing and provides ample space below the wing for external stores. In the US aircraft all the offensive load is in practice hung under the pivoted wings despite the need for all the pylons to pivot to stay aligned with the airflow. This was not attempted by the MiG OKB, partly

Below: Today the original Ye-231 is preserved in the VVS (air force) museum at Monino. Many of its features are similar or even identical to those of today's MiG-23s, though it never carried armament. Very similar MiG-23S and SM aircraft were built in small series and saw combat duty with the VVS.

because of the immediate (but not insoluble) difficulty of fitting swivelling pylons, coupled with the fact that in the Soviet aircraft adequate pylon capacity could be provided on the fuselage and fixed wing gloves.

As described in the next chapter, the main carry-through box lies in the top of the fuselage and extends across the fuselage proper (which vanishes upstream of this point) and the capacious rectangular side portions, and then tapers off to hold the wing pivot near the outer edge of the fixed wing glove. The pivot holds the wing very firmly via a triangular extension to the main torsion box on the inner end of the forged root rib. Ahead of this is another strong machined forging in the form of a horn which determines the sweep angle. The tip of the horn is connected to a universal joint on the end of irreversible screwjack driven by twin hydraulic motors. Either motor can position the wings, but at half the normal speed. The range of sweep angle is an arc of 56° though only three settings are available: 16°, 45° or 72°. The latter angle aligns the leading edge with that of the fixed glove section.

At minimum sweep, ie maximum span, severe limitations are imposed on the IAS (indicated air-

MIKOYAN MiG-23MF FLOGGER-G CUTAWAY DRAWING KEY

1. Pitot tube.
2. Radome.
3. Flat dish radar scanner.
4. Scanner tracking mechanism.
5. 'High Lark' J-band pulse Doppler radar module.
6. 'Swift-Rod' ILS aerial.
7. Radar mounting bulkhead.
8. Cooling air scoop.
9. Ventral Doppler navigation aerial
10. Weapons system avionics equipment.
11. Nose compartment access doors.
12. Yaw vane.
13. Dynamic pressure probe (q-feel)
14. SRO-2 'Odd Rods' IFF antenna.
15. Temperature probe.
16. Cockpit front pressure bulkhead.
17. Sensitive IR° detector.
18. Nosewheel steering control.
19. Torque scissor links.
20. Pivoted axle beam.
21. Twin aft-retracting nosewheels.
22. Nosewheel spray/debris guards.
23. Shock absorber strut.
24. Nosewheel doors.·
25. Doppler blister (behind, nosewheel retraction jack).
26. Angle of attack transmitter.
27. Rudder pedals.

28. Control column.
29. Three-position wing sweep control lever.
30. Engine throttle lever.
31. Cockpit section framing.
32. Ejection seat firing handles.
33. Radar 'head-down' display.
34. Instrument panel.
35. Instrument panel shroud.
36. Weapons sighting unit 'head-up' display.
37. Armoured glass windscreen panel.
38. K-13A (AA-2 *Atoll*) infra-red homing.
39. Missile launch rail.
40. AA-2-2 *Advanced Atoll* radar homing AAM.
41. Wing glove pylon.
42. Cockpit canopy cover, upward hingeing.
43. Electrically heated rear view mirror.
44. Pilot's 'zero-zero' ejection seat.
45. Ejection seat headrest/drogue parachute container.

46. Canopy hinge point.
47. Canopy hydraulic jack.
48. Boundary layer splitter plate.
49. Boundary layer ramp bleed air holes.
50. Port engine air intake.
51. Adjustable intake ramp screw jack control.
52. Intake internal flow fences.
53. Retractable landing/taxying lamp, port and starboard.
54. Pressure sensor, automatic intake control system.
55. Variable area intake ramp doors.
56. Intake duct framing.
57. Ventral cannon ammunition magazine.
58. Control rod linkages.
59. Intake ramp bleed air ejector.
60. Boundary layer spill duct.
61. Avionics equipment.
62. ADF sense aerial.

63. Tailplane control rods.
64. Forward fuselage fuel tanks.
65. Wing glove fairing.
66. Intake duct suction relief doors.
67. Ground power and intercomm sockets.
68. Twin missile carrier/launch unit.
69. Port fuselage stores pylon.
70. Weapons system electronic control units.
71. Electronic counter-measures equipment.
72. Wing glove pylon attachment fitting.
73. SO-69 'Sirena-3' radar warning and suppression aerials.
74. Wing sweep control horn.
75. Screw jack wing sweep rotary actuator.
76. Twin hydraulic motors.

77. Central combining gearbox.
78. Wing pivot box carry-through unit (welded steel construction).
79. Pivot box integral fuel tank.
80. VHF aerial.
81. Wing pivot bearing.
82. Starboard 'Sirena-3' radar warning and suppression aerials.
83. Extended-chord sawtooth leading edge.
84. Fixed portion of leading edge.
85. Non-swivelling, jettisionable wing pylon (wing restricted to forward swept position).
86. Jettisonable fuel tank (176gal/800lit capacity).
87. Nose section of MiG-23U *Flogger-C* tandem seat trainer.
88. Student pilot's cockpit.
89. Folding blind flying hood.

90. Rear seat periscope, extended.
91. Instructor's cockpit.
92. MiG-23BN *Flogger-F* dedicated ground attack variant.
93. Doppler radar
94. Laser ranger and masked-target seeker (below).
95. Raised cockpit canopy.
96. Armoured fuselage side panels.
97. Starboard wing leading edge flap (lowered)
98. Leading edge flap hydraulic actuator.
99. Starboard wing integral fuel tank (total fuel capacity 1,265gal/5,750lit).
100. Starboard nagivation light.

101. Wing fully forward.
102. Static discharger.
103. Full-span 3-segment plain flap (lowered).
104. Starboard wing intermediate (45° sweep) position.
105. Starboard wing full (72° sweep) position.
106. Two-segment spoilers/lift dumpers (open).
107. Spoiler hydraulic actuators.
108. Flap hydraulic jack.
109. Wing glove flexible seal.
110. Flap mechanical interconnection and disengage mechanism.
111. Wing root housing.
112. Dorsal spine fairing.
113. Engine intake compressor face.
114. Wing root housing sealing plate.
115. Rear fuselage fuel tanks.
116. Tailplane control linkages.
117. Fin root fillet.
118. Afterburner duct cooling air scoop.
119. Artificial feel control units.
120. Control system hydraulic accumulator.
121. Artificial feel and autopilot controls.

139. Variable-area afterburner nozzle.
140. Fixed taileron tab.
141. Honeycomb core trailing edge panel.
142. Static discharger.
143. Port all-moving taileron construction.
144. Afterburner nozzle control jacks (6).
145. Taileron pivot bearing.
146. Taileron power unit.
147. Airbrakes (4) upper and lower surfaces.
148. Airbrake hydraulic jacks.
149. Afterburner duct heat shroud.
150. Ventral fin, folded (landing gear down) position.
151. Ventral fin down position.
152. Screw jack fin actuator.
153. Fin attachment fuselage main frame.
154. Double frame for removal of rear fuselage for access to Tumansky R-29B afterburning turbojet, with water injection.
155. Lower UHF aerial.
156. Engine accessory equipment compartment.
157. Air-conditioning system equipment.
158. Port plain flap.
159. Spoiler actuators.
160. Port spoilers/lift dumpers.
161. Flap guide rails.
162. Fixed spoiler strips.
163. Static discharger.
164. Wing tip fairing.
165. Port navigation light.
166. Port leading edge flap.
167. Leading-edge flap control linkage.
168. Front spar.
169. Wing rib construction.
170. Rear spar.
171. Auxiliary centre gear.
172. Wing skin support struts.
173. Port wing integral fuel tank.
174. Wing pylon attachment fitting.
175. Leading-edge rib construction.
176. Port mainwheel.
177. Mainwheel door/debris guard.
178. Shock absorber strut.
179. Pivoted axle beam.
180. Articulated mainwheel leg strut.
181. Mainwheel leg doors.
182. R-60 (AA-8 *Aphid*) short range AAM
183. GSh-23L twin-barrel 23mm cannon.
184. Ventral cannon pack.
185. Gun gas venting air scoop.
186. Fuselage centreline pylon.
187. Auxiliary fuel tank (176gal/800lit capacity), for centreline pylon (also see 86).
188. *Apex* missile launch rail.
189. Launch rail attachment hardpoints.
190. R-23R (AA-7 *Apex*) medium-range AAM.

122. Taileron trim controls.
123. Starboard all-moving taileron.
124. Fin leading edge.
125. Tailfin construction.
126. Short-wave ground control communications aerial.
127. Fin tip UHF aerial fairing
128. ILS aerial.
129. ECM aerial.
130. 'Sirena-3' SO-69 tail warning radar (five receiver aerials).
131. Tail nagivation light (beneath SO-69 pod).
132. Static discharger.
133. Rudder.
134. Honeycomb core construction.
135. Rudder hydraulic power units, port and starboard.
136. Parachute release links.
137. Brake parachute housing.
138. Split conic fairing parachute doors.

AVIAGRAPHICA

speed) and the loading that can be imparted in dive pull-outs or tight turns. There are no movable surfaces on the glove, unlike the American F-111 and F-14 which have powerful "glove vanes" of different kinds and the IDS version of Tornado which has a Krüger flap. The MiG-23 is rare in having a glove without a movable surface, and this quite small portion of wing has an effect on lift and trim out of all proportion to its size. In contrast, the pivoting outer panels have movable surfaces along both the leading and trailing edges. On the leading edge the inner portion is fixed. In the original Ye-231 prototypes this section became aligned with the fixed glove at maximum sweep, but in the course of development the chord was greatly increased, terminating at the inboard end in a giant dogtooth discontinuity. This jagged forward-pointing portion creates a powerful vortex at high angles of attack (for example, when pulling g in a tight turn) with the wings fully swept and with the dogtooth well away from the glove. This vortex scrubs back across the wing, re-energizing the airflow and maintaining the maximum effectiveness from the spoilers downstream.

There are two sections of spoiler, inboard and outboard, in the upper surface of each outer wing. In flight they operate independently to help roll the aircraft, operating in conjunction with the left and right tailerons. A taileron is a tailplane (US, horizontal stabilizer) which is used not only as the primary control in pitch but also for roll. There are no ailerons, the MiG-23 being rolled solely by the tailerons working differentially (left one way, and right the other) in combination with opening of either the left or right spoilers. After landing, all four spoilers flick fully open together to increase drag and, especially, to destroy residual wing lift and thus, by putting much more weight on the main wheels, make the brakes more effective.

Slotted flaps

The third set of wing surfaces is the flaps. These are of the slotted type, made like all movable surfaces on these aircraft of aluminium honeycomb. Like the wing panels, LE flaps and spoilers, they are driven hydraulically, in this case by linear jacks. At mini-

Below: A MiG-23MF Flogger-G in the circuit at low speed. To pull into a tight turn the spoilers on the starboard wing are open and the tailerons asymmetrically at negative incidence.

mum sweep the three sections of flap on each wing are all usable; at the intermediate setting the two outer sections remain operative, and at maximum sweep the outermost flap section can still be used. In the early days of the MiG-23 failure of the wing sweep actuator was not uncommon. The correct drill was to eject, and on one occasion when the experienced pilot elected to land the aircraft he was killed. Reliability today is certainly higher, though probably still inferior to that of Western VG fighters.

The MiG OKB and TsAGI were mindful of their experience with the MiG-21 where the size of the fin had to be increased on three separate occasions in order to achieve satisfactory directional stability. With the MiG-23 the vertical tail was made very large at the start, and extended fowards with a giant dorsal fin extending half-way to the cockpit. Moreover, a ventral fin was added, and, because this would have fouled the runway on takeoff and landing, this is hinged to a fixed root section and arranged to fold sideways. Whenever the landing gear is selected down, the ventral fin is hydraulically rotated round to the right to the horizontal position. When the gear is selected up, the fin pivots down—much faster than the gear retraction—and locks in its vertical position, giving excellent stability. The MiG-23 fin area has never had to be increased; indeed many recent aircraft have a *smaller* dorsal fin!

Flogger-A goes into service

All the early Ye-231 prototypes, flown in the mid-1960s, were powered by the Lyul'ka AL-7F-1 engine, a quite old but outstanding turbojet notable for its smoky trail at full throttle. The first of these aircraft—with 231 painted on it, and today preserved in the VVS Museum at Monino—gave a spirited display at the last Soviet Aviation Day at Moscow Domodyedovo airport on 9 July 1967. The pilot, chief OKB test pilot Aleksandr Fedotov, swept the wings to and fro at speeds estimated from 250 to 500mph (400-800km/h), whilst making rapid manoeuvres in the rolling plane. Clearly there was not much wrong with the basic machine, unlike the prototypes of the F-111, and sufficient of this model were built to equip a complete regiment numbering about 75 aircraft, plus about 25 in reserve. This aircraft was dubbed Flogger-A by NATO, and the production machines had weapon pylons and were

able to fly combat missions. Nevertheless, a major redesign was in prospect, not (as some Western writers have claimed) because of "serious stability and control problems" but simply in order to fit a completely new engine.

This engine is the Tumanskii R-27, designed some eight years later than the AL-7, though broadly similar in its elegant simplicity and robust design. Fractionally more powerful than the older engine, and appreciably more fuel-efficient, it differed most markedly in being less than two-thirds the size and only 60 per cent as heavy. In order to install this shorter and lighter engine the basic Ye-231 design had to be substantially modified, the engine being moved forward slightly (but carried on frames at the original stations), the rear fuselage shortened by 1.06m (42in), and the wings moved forward 0.61m (24in) on smaller fixed gloves. At the same time the outer-wing chord was increased, and the dogteeth added. All this restored the centre of gravity and centre of pressure relationship, reduced structure weight, and also reduced drag. An incidental change was more rapid spool-up of the engine, going from idle to full afterburner in 4.5 seconds, and without visible smoke.

An accompanying cutaway drawing shows the location of the impressive internal fuel capacity of 5,750 litres (1,265 Imp gal, 1,519 US gal). Roughly half is in the main torsion boxes forming the structural core of each outer wing, these being sealed integral tanks. The rest is in integral and flexible cell-type tanks in the fuselage, disposed equally ahead of and behind the wing surrounding the engine and its inlet duct, and inside the carry-through box.

Phantom-type inlet

The MiG OKB had used lateral inlets before, but never complicated inlets for use at Mach 2 or more. Designing them took a lot of effort, despite using the F-4 Phantom inlet as a basis, but today they seem quite routine. Each inlet is vertical, having the section of a pure rectangle with rounded outer corners. Its inner edge is a splitter plate whose leading edge stands about 4in (100mm) away from the fuselage. The plate has a wedge form in plan view, and aft-facing exits at top and bottom suck away the turbulent boundary layer through several hundred fine holes in the outer wall of the plate. Boundary layer from the forward fuselage, passing through the gap inboard of the plate, is divided by a horizontal wedge into lower and upper flows dumped overboard below and above the fuselage. Inside the inlet are two horizontal guide vanes and a variable-profile inner wall positioned automatically by screwjacks. Almost immediately the duct curves inwards to meet its partner on the opposite side to form a single circular duct under the wing carry-through box. To admit extra air on takeoff two rectangular suck-in doors are provided in the outer skin under the wing glove, communicating with similar doors in the duct wall.

Tail details

The horizontal tails have already been described, but an important aerodynamic feature is that, in sharp contrast to the F-111, there is a large gap between the wing and tailplanes even with the wing fully swept back. Apart from this the aerodynamics are very similar, the horizontal tails being located a few inches lower than the level of the trailing edge of the wing. Of course, as the wing sweeps back, the rear inboard portion has to be accommodated inside the fuselage, and it enters between precisely tailored upper and lower hinged lips of thin sheet with Teflon edges. The vertical tail is conventional apart from the fact that the rudder is driven by left and right pairs of small actuators, the pair being in separate hydraulic systems. In contrast, each taileron (half tailplane) is driven by a single large electro-hydraulic power unit, and unlike the MiG-21 (whose tailplane actuator is far away in the fin) the output ram drives the surface directly, from below.

Soviet requirements have for many years been rigorous in their demand for powerful airbrakes on all combat aircraft, meeting severe numerical capabilities and having no noticeable effect on aircraft pitch attitude or trim at any airspeed. They also have to be able to blow back against hydraulic pressure as airspeed increases. Sometimes, as in the MiG-21, airbrakes are a continuing problem, but in the past 25 years it has become usual to position the airbrakes above and below the extreme tail. Where there is a single fin and mid-set tailplanes this means four airbrakes, and this arrangement was pioneered by Sukhoi's S-2 and T-3 of early 1956. Since then the four-petal configuration has seldom given any trouble, and it was one of the features of the Ye-231 series that worked well from the start, despite the surfaces being moved bodily forward in relation to the tail surfaces with the switch to the R-27 engine.

Poor all-round pilot view

Of course, one feature of the F-111 left severely alone is the ejectable crew capsule. All MiG-23s have a conventional ejection seat, usually a standard model in the KM-1 series. The canopy is typically Soviet, much smaller than in Western fighters and giving the pilot little spare headroom and not much rear vision except via the mirror overhead. It appears to be Soviet policy to rate reduction in drag as more important than all-round pilot view, and like most other Soviet tactical aircraft the top of the canopy is level with the fuselage downstream. The canopy is hinged at the rear and opened upwards by a hydraulic jack. The front windscreen is fixed and bulletproof. As noted later, the forward view is improved in specialized attack models.

The R-27 is a basically simple turbojet in typical Tumanskii tradition. It is installed in a tight tunnel in the rear and centre fuselage, the HP spool and combustion section being surrounded by the rear fuel tank. Accessories are underneath, accessible through eight doors on the underside of the fuselage. The four bottom doors are perforated by 50mm (2in) holes to prevent internal pressure build-up

Below: The main landing gears of all aircraft of this family are an object-lesson in robust yet simple design, giving wide track, long travel for rough surfaces and (especially in the MiG-27) low footprint pressure, yet folding into small boxes outboard of the engine air duct.

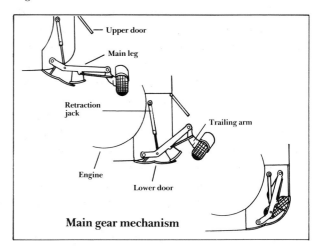

Above: Head-on view of the landing gear of a Flogger-G on a foreign goodwill visit. The fighter versions, unlike the MiG-27 dedicated attack models, are designed to operate from runways.

from various ram inlets (including leakage from the main inlet) and improve cooling. For all-round access, and for changing the engine, the complete rear fuselage and tail is removed by unbolting the No 28-28B double frame (see item 154 in the cutaway on pages 8 and 9).

Rugged, simple landing gears

Typical of Soviet military hardware, the landing gears are bold, tough and highly effective. A British magazine described the main units as "decidedly complex", but in fact they could hardly be simpler, and they fold into a remarkably small space whilst leaving the underside of the fuselage free for long centreline stores. The design is unusual in that on the ground each J-shaped main leg is horizontal. A high-strength steel tube, it is pivoted at its inner end close to the centreline of the aircraft and prevented from folding upwards by the trapped fluid in the massive vertical retraction jack. This provides a little shock absorption, but the main springing is provided by the trailing levers which carry the wheels and have their own shock-absorber struts. Upon retraction the main leg is pulled almost straight up, and slightly back, the trailing link being folded down and forwards by a tie rod until the wheel is stowed almost horizontal in the bottom of the fuselage. The bay is closed by two simple doors hinged to the fuselage and two smaller plates carried on the gear itself.

A particularly neat feature is that one of the doors encloses the upper half of the extended wheel, where it forms a very effective guard against mud, stones, slush and other debris which would otherwise be distributed liberally over the underside of the wings and fuselage. Frontal Aviation knows better than NATO that military pilots must get used to operating away from airfields, and the MiG-23 family, especially the attack versions, is designed for sustained operations from unpaved surfaces. For this reason the nose gear has an even more prominent mudguard covering the upper rear quarter of the two wheels that are used to spread the load. This unit is vertical when extended, and is long enough to give most versions of the aircraft a nose-up attitude on the ground. The leg has a long stroke and is hydraulically steerable via the cockpit pedals which are immediately above. Like the main units, retraction is also hydraulic, in this case to the rear. A cruciform braking parachute is housed in the tube above the rear fuselage.

Development of other versions

In the development of the MiG-23 for service in 1967-73 all priority was on the interceptor version. Pacing items on this aircraft were the new engine, the radar and two new species of AAM which have since been used on other types of aircraft. While this very important fighter was being readied for service, production began of further versions. The most immediate was the MiG-23U dual-control trainer. Next in timing came the specialized attack MiG-27, followed by the hybrid MiG-23BN, both of which have totally different avionics and weapons. At quite an early stage the R-27 engine was replaced by the improved and more powerful R-29, changing the designation of the fighter to MiG-23MF. A version of the same engine, with a shorter and simpler afterburner, powers the attack versions. In general, standard Soviet aircraft of these versions have also been supplied to Warsaw Pact air forces, as outlined in the final section of this book. For countries outside the Warsaw Pact somewhat simpler and less-capable versions have been developed, most notably a downgraded interceptor fitted with the same nose as the trainer.

More recently, further developed versions of both the interceptor and the attack version have been produced in large numbers, and one of the former, with only minor downgrading in avionic fit, has been exported outside the Warsaw Pact. In addition, one of the latest attack versions is being manufactured under licence by Hindustan Aeronautics in India.

3
Technical Features

THOUGH THE Ye-23 family has been developed along two distinct mainstreams, one dedicated to air combat and the other to attack on surface targets, all members use basically the same airframe. Long familiarity with these aircraft tends to obscure their considerable capability, the keys to which are variable sweep and an engine of exceptional power. These qualities have been used to achieve very high speeds at all flight levels, and to lift loads of avionics and weapons several times greater than anything possible with the MiG-21 and which compare well with those of contemporary Western aircraft.

This chapter opens with a brief look at basic mission parameters, and it is at once seen that they differ considerably for the two main versions. The most obvious difference is the shorter range of the attack aircraft, and this is due to its choice of a lo (low-level) profile and heavy load of weapons. Taking this version first, it needs a longer run than the fighter. Rather misleadingly, *Jane's* quotes the respective takeoff runs as: fighter 900m (2,950ft), attack 800m (2,625ft). Looking closer we find the latter figure is at a weight of 15,700kg (34,600lb), almost five tons below the maximum. With maximum fuel and weapons the run is about 1900m (6,230ft) despite the excellent lift coefficient of the wing.

Versatility of the VG wing

Opponents of the variable-sweep wing claim that a "simpler" or "lighter" alternative is to use variable aerofoil profile by means of drooping leading edge flaps (as on the F-16 and F-18) or powerful slats, combined with manoeuvre-capable flaps on the trailing edge. This argument overlooks the fact that this kind of tinkering with the wing's cross-section can be done even more beneficially with a VG wing, and the latter has a particularly powerful effect in tailoring the wing to the requirements of flight at highly supersonic Mach numbers. In particular, the 72° setting of the MiG-23 series matches the aircraft to the attack run on a surface target at full throttle at just above ground level. This cannot be flown by aircraft with fixed-geometry wings without severe structural stresses and extreme discomfort (to the risk of incapacitation) to the pilot.

Little has been published in the West about the navigation aids of the attack versions, but there seems little doubt that the primary aid must be inertial. Like the fighter versions a doppler radar is carried under the nose, but avionics details are discussed in the next two chapters. The point is that the attack version is equipped to fly at full power with maximum bomb load at low level, with the wings fully swept. In contrast, the fighter generally operates at lighter weights in thinner air, though it can fly faster and probably pulls more g in combat manoeuvres.

Fighter mission profiles

The profile portrayed for the fighter mission is, of course, just one of many. In some situations even the fighter may be tasked to fly the whole mission at low level, and this would severely curtail the range. On the other hand, while the attack versions can carry bombs on the centreline, the fighter almost always has a tank in this position and thus tends to have basically greater operating radius. Two simple graphs plot the way the weight of the aircraft reduces as the mission is flown out to the limit of its radius and then back to base. It will be seen that release of the external bomb/missile load from the attack aircraft has a very large and sudden effect, whereas with the fighter the main characteristic is the progressive burn-off of fuel on the long out and return parts of the mission. In each case, of course, use of afterburner sharply increases the slope of the line, ie of the rate at which the fuel is burned.

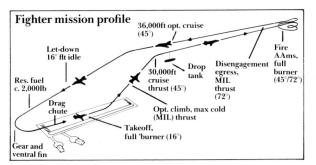

Fighter mission profile

36,000ft opt. cruise (45°)

Let-down 16°flt idle

Fire AAms, full burner (45°/72°)

30,000ft cruise thrust (45°)

Drop tank

Disengagement egress, MIL thrust (72°)

Res. fuel c. 2,000lb

Drag chute

Opt. climb, max cold (MIL) thrust

Takeoff, full 'burner (16°)

Gear and ventral fin

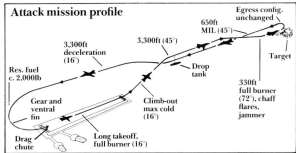

Attack mission profile

3,300ft deceleration (16°)

3,300ft (45°)

650ft MIL (45°)

Egress config. unchanged

Target

Res. fuel c. 2,000lb

Gear and ventral fin

Drop tank

330ft full burner (72°), chaff flares, jammer

Drag chute

Climb-out max cold (16°)

Long takeoff, full burner (16°)

Above: A simple representation of a MiG-23 fighter mission. Most of the flight is at high altitude, giving reduced fuel burn as shown by the gentle slopes of the lines in the diagram at the foot of the page. The symbolic airbase is shown with two hardened aircraft shelters off the parallel taxiway.

Above: For comparison, this is a schematic representation of a typical mission by a MiG-27 attack aircraft. Though the radius of action looks the same, it is in fact only about one-third as great, because of the need to fly at low level with a heavy bomb load. Note the longer take-off run.

Right: This diagram plots the attack mission in another way (two different radii of action are shown, with different bomb loads). For the explanation, see caption below.

Two other technical graphs, in each case referring to the fighter versions, show basic features of air-combat performance. One is the plot of maximum attainable level speed against height. In maximum dry (so-called MIL, or military) thrust the graph is a plain continuous curve peaking at just beyond the speed of sound (Mach 1) between 6,000 and 12,000m (about 20,000-40,000ft) altitude, and with a sea-level limit a little over Mach 0.9. In full afterburner it is a different story. The maximum speed is a clearly defined peak at well beyond Mach 2 at a little over 10,000m (32,800ft). Such a speed cannot be reached at any other height. Above this level the falling air density results in reduced engine thrust and greater wing AOA (angle of attack), while at lower levels the aircraft is structurally limited until at

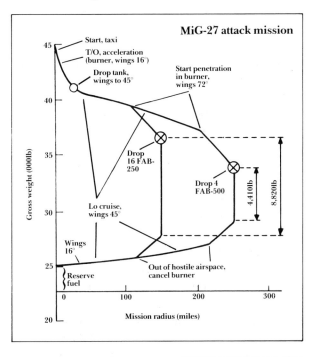

MiG-27 attack mission

Start, taxi

T/O, acceleration (burner, wings 16°)

Drop tank, wings to 45°

Start penetration in burner, wings 72°

Drop 16 FAB-250

Drop 4 FAB-500

4,410lb

8,820lb

Lo cruise, wings 45°

Wings 16°

Reserve fuel

Out of hostile airspace, cancel burner

Gross weight (000lb)

Mission radius (miles)

Right: This diagram plots the way the weight of the MiG-23MF falls away in the course of a typical fighter mission. At the top (radius zero) the aircraft takes off at maximum gross weight of 40,670lb (18,900kg). This weight initially falls very rapidly, as the aircraft climbs out in full afterburner at high weight in dense air. Climbing into colder, thinner air, and coming out of afterburner makes a great difference to rate of fuel burn. In combat fuel burn rises suddenly as burner is engaged, and the four black dots represent points at which an AAM is fired. In the attack diagram (above) the two bombloads are respectively 8,8821lb and 4,410lb (4,000 and 2,000kg).

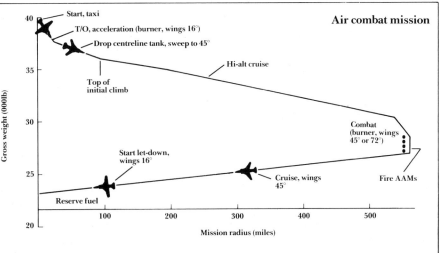

Start, taxi

T/O, acceleration (burner, wings 16°)

Drop centreline tank, sweep to 45°

Hi-alt cruise

Top of initial climb

Combat (burner, wings 45° or 72°)

Start let-down, wings 16°

Cruise, wings 45°

Fire AAMs

Reserve fuel

Gross weight (000lb)

Mission radius (miles)

Air combat mission

Right: A graphical plot showing how the maximum speed of the MiG-23MF fighter varies in three flight regimes from sea level up to the aircraft's ceiling. In MIL (maximum dry thrust, ie without afterburner) the speed never quite equals Mach 1. In full afterburner the maximum speed rises steadily with increasing altitude, reaching a maximum near the tropopause at about 36,000ft (11,000m). Above this height all performance falls away increasingly rapidly. The ceiling of 61,000ft (18,600m) is reached at around Mach 1.8 in the clean condition (without any AAMs or external fuel). Ceiling in MIL thrust can be seen to be around 48,000ft (14,630m).

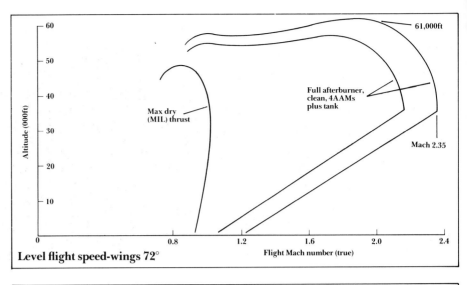

Level flight speed-wings 72°

Right: Similar performance plots showing maximum possible rate of sustained turn (in degrees per second) at all heights. The curves are for one flight regime only, with four air-to-air missiles but no tanks, in full afterburner and with the wings set at the optimum sweep angle (which varies according to altitude). At any chosen height the plot rises to a maximum (subsonic at sea level, well over Mach 1 at 35,000ft/10,670m and then falling back again). At sea level the curve is sharply peaked, reaching a very high turn rate at about Mach 0.7. At high altitudes the peak is very flat, because turn rate is low at all speeds. Obviously, at the ceiling (61,000ft/18,590m) the turn rate is zero.

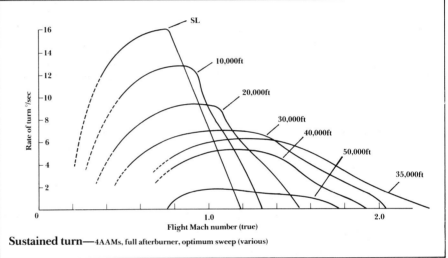

Sustained turn—4AAMs, full afterburner, optimum sweep (various)

sea level the maximum speed is only just over Mach 1 (about 1.2 in the clean condition). Separate curves are shown for the clean and fully armed aircraft, the latter suffering the drag and weight of its external stores.

The final graph is the usual mapping of maximum sustained turn against attainable flight Mach number. As the MiG-23 is a variable-sweep aircraft the curves for each flight level are sometimes visibly kinked, change in sweep resulting in a better performance than could be achieved by a fixed-geometry fighter. In general, the greater rates of turn and the higher Mach numbers are all achieved with the wings at 72° sweep, while at higher altitudes the best results are with intermediate settings. In any case, it will be seen that at each flight level there is one clearly defined Mach number at which the

sustained turn rate is a maximum. At all heights in excess of 6,000m (20,000ft) the best sustained turn rate is achieved at speeds in excess of Mach 1. As might be expected, turn rate falls off inexorably all the way from sea level to the aircraft ceiling, as the air density is reduced. At the clean ceiling of some 18,500m (61,000ft) the sustained turn rate is zero.

Accompanying photographs show some close-up details common to all versions. One shows the underside of the starboard (right-hand) main wing pivot. It is noteworthy that the skin downstream is streaked with oil which has seeped out from the large-diameter steel pivot. Where possible, Western practice has been to use pivots with Teflon bearings needing no lubrication. In the MiGs the steel carry-through box forms an integral tank, and the seepage of kerosene may make sealing problems more dif-

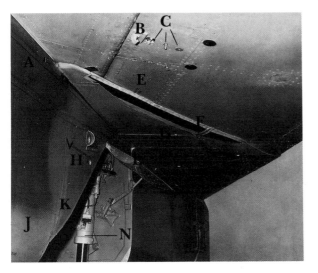

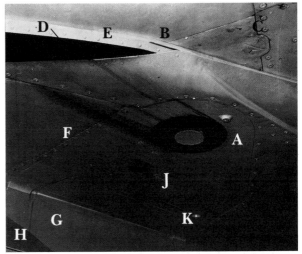

Above: Looking up at the right (starboard) wing root of a Flogger-G: A, polythene-edged hinged flap; B, rear pylon lug; C, pylon service connectors; D, pylon mount; E, spoiler power units access; F, sprung flexible seal; G, glove; H, injection water connector, 28 litres; J, engine accessory access door; K, Fuselage Stn. 22; L, upper main-gear door; M, auxiliary inlets ground cover (removed for flight); N, main-gear retraction jack. All subsequent detail photographs are of Flogger-Gs.

Above: A closer view of the starboard wing pivot, the location of which is evident from the photograph on the left: A, pivot; B, pivoting outer wing (in 72° fully swept position); C, main spar and skin joint; D, rubber flexible seal; E, aluminium edge pressed up against wing; F, edge of wing carry-through box; G, side of fuselage; H, main landing-gear upper bay door; J, fuel system drain connector (in carry-through box tank sump); K, hydraulic jacking point for lifting aircraft.

ficult. In early Western cutaways of these aircraft there was inevitably some incorrect guesswork, and a common error was to place the wing sweep actuator behind the carry-through box. In fact, as noted earlier, each wing is positioned by a horn projecting from the forward part of the forged root rib, driven by irreversible screwjacks powered through a central combiner gearbox by the two hydraulic motors. In the early days, complete mechanical failure of the drive was not uncommon. One Indian pilot, on a MiG-21 conversion course at Tashkent (Uzbekistan), noticed two MiG-23 wing-sweep failures at the same air base during his visit, one pilot ejecting and the other being killed.

Attachment for long-range tank

Two of the close-ups show the attachments for the wing pylon. This has seldom been fitted, and is used chiefly to carry auxiliary fuel tanks for long-range ferrying. As it does not swivel, it is usable only with the wings set at 16° sweep. Curiously, these pylons are omitted from almost every description of the MiG-23 family published in the West.

The underside of the junction between the fixed wing glove and the pivoted outer wing is also shown in photographs. The trailing edge of the glove is

fitted with a stiff and heavy strip of rubberized fabric moulded into a curve so that its free (rear) edge is always pressed up against the wing. This edge carries an aluminium strip edged with Teflon. On MiG-23s seen by the author the seal has been excellent, and it is probably replaced every 250 hours or so. The fuselage box which accepts the rear inboard section of the wing and flap is sealed under the wing by a

Below: Looking aft under the same area: A, limit of fixed glove; B, dogtooth (aerial?); C, SO-69 RWR aerial; D, wing at 72°; E, fixed pylon fitting; F, box housing wing-root seal plate; G, taileron root; H, water filler; J, inspection hatch; K, hydraulic lines; L, fuel pipes; M, Station 7, tank No 2.

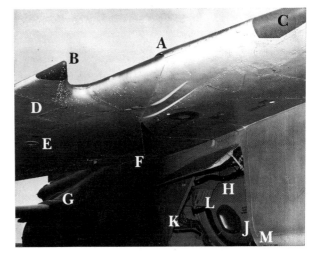

long aluminium plate with a Teflon upper edge. This plate is pivoted at its forward end and pressed upwards by springs. When the wing is at maximum sweep the plate is pushed fully down, against the springs, into a box which projects no less than 40mm from the side of the fuselage.

The photograph which best shows this box also gives a close-up of the dielectric (glassfibre insulating) areas which cover electronics aerials on the wing dogtooth and on the leading edge of the glove. The latter cover the two forward-facing passive receiver aerials in the SO-69 Sirena 3 RWR (radar warning receiver) system. This automatically detects any hostile radar signal, and not only warns the pilot that his aircraft is being tracked but also gives the direction of the enemy radar. Each forward aerial covers a sector from dead ahead to 110° to left or right. The function of the aerials on the tips of the dogteeth is not known to the author. Clearly, if these are in any way directional, their angular coverage must vary according to the sweep angle of the wings.

The same picture shows items inside the right-hand main landing-gear bay. The absence of clutter is remarkable, but it is possible to see an array of hydraulic pipes and an accumulator, a fuel pipe and, at the top, the shiny black water filling pipe. The fact that (so far as is known) almost all the modern Tumanskii engines use water injection on takeoff is another thing usually omitted from Western descriptions of Soviet aircraft. The inner wall of the bay is the engine air duct. The circular cover (which on the particular aircraft photographed bore the number 10655) can be unbolted to provide a direct view of the front of the engine immediately downstream. The stencilled label says "inspection of compressor guide vanes", though this engine has none!

Several accompanying photographs show the small numbers identifying various fuselage stations, almost all of which are at major structural frames. In Western aircraft it has been usual to identify all stations throughout the airframe according to a precise distance (in inches or millimetres), from a reference point, but in Soviet aircraft the stations have a plain number. In these aircraft Stations 28 and 28B together form the double frame at which the rear fuselage and tail is disconnected. Today removal of the entire rear fuselage is rare in Western fighters, but it is common in MiG and Sukhoi designs as a means of facilitating access to the hot parts of the

Above: The right underside of the rear fuselage: A, Fuselage Station 28/28A (structural break); B, hatch giving access to main structural disconnection; C, hydraulic unit; D, "before opening hatch unscrew two bolts fastening duct"; E, engine hatch; F, air holes; G, engine autocontrol electrics; H, open doors; J, "disconnect hydraulic valves"; K, DC generator, AC generator; L, electronic warfare Reper-M antenna (both sides of aircraft); M, liquid drains; N, fixed underfin nose.

engine and of changing the whole engine if necessary. To remove the tail more than 20 electric, electronic, air, fuel, drain and hydraulic couplings have to be disconnected, quite apart from the major structural joints.

As already noted each half-tailplane is a taileron able to control the aircraft in roll as well as in pitch. Like the rudder, most of each taileron is a honeycomb structure, with a beautifully smooth surface. Much of the rest of the airframe has spot-welded skin, though numerous kinds of rivets, countersunk screws and bolts are also to be seen. The inner end of the taileron is kinked to accommodate a pivot axis spigot swept sharply backwards and parallel with the surface's main spar. Inevitably this arrangement necessitates a substantial fixed inboard portion which, in effect, reduces the size of the surface. In early three views, and plastic model kits, not only are the tailerons pivoted at right-angles but they have straight inboard ends adjacent to the fuselage!

In about 1977 the inboard trailing edge of each taileron was extended by bonding on an extra strip. This is not a ground-adjustable tab, and apart from slightly increasing the power of the surface their purpose is unknown.

The upper part of the vertical tail is extremely neat, the one puzzle (on the MiG-23MF Flogger-G

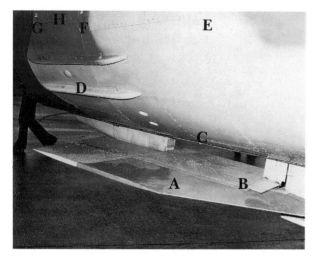

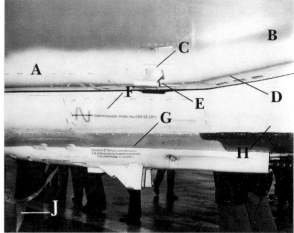

Above: Whenever the landing gear is selected down, the underfin is folded over to the right side to enable it to clear the ground. This shows the surface on a parked aircraft: A, underfin (folded); B, fin actuator hinge fairing door; C, drain pipe terminating under jet nozzle; D, lower right airbrake (one of four) in closed position, showing twin axial bracing and hinge fairings and central blister over jack fitting; E, Station 30; F, Station 31; G, Station 32; H, taileron power unit access.

Above: The area around the GSh-23L gun: A, AAM subsystem access panel; B, inlet electrothermal deicer element; C, venturi and pressure sensor (air inlet control system); D, ramp bleed ejectors; E, retractable landing/taxi light (both sides of aircraft); F, gun inspection and SAU-23/ARZ controls and ammunition access; G, "Attention ! Before removing GSh-23L loosen four bolts fastening case ejector to gun mount"; H, steel anti-blast skin; J, warning flag, aux. inlet ground covers.

aircraft that made goodwill visits to Finland and France in 1978) being that the entire fin cap appears to be metal, with numerous rows of pan-head rivets indicating numerous internal ribs. It is universally assumed that aircraft of this family have a very large fin cap moulded in glassfibre and covering communications aerials which could not operate inside a metal skin. It will be seen that the rudder is driven by pairs of extremely small and simple hydraulic jacks without any visible feedback or control linkage. The actuators are pivoted behind the fin rear spar, and inclined out to left and right to drive the rudder from opposite sides.

A feature often overlooked is that the chord of the rudder is greater (by about 40mm, 1.6in) than the chord of the top of the fin. The upper edge of the rudder has a small doubler reinforcement, and the sweptback hinge causes a slight bulge in the fin. At the rear of the fin tip are the usual devices, the most complex being the SO-69 Sirena 3 RWR installation contained in a streamlined pod. The main passive receivers, in the form of small spiral helix aerials, are mounted diagonally on each side of this fairing, where they cover a 110° sector from dead astern to abeam. Above this, and thus seemingly able to reflect radar signals confusingly into the SO-69 receivers, is the extraordinary ILS aerial system which in most

MiG-23 type aircraft is repeated under the nose, each aerial covering the forward or rear hemisphere. The undernose aerial is used during an ILS approach, the other being for back-beam departures.

Below: Top of the vertical tail: A, Swift Rod ILS (instrument landing system) aerial; B, SO-69 Sirena 3 RWR pod; C, ECM jammer transmitter (both sides): D, SO-69 antenna access; E, navigation light; F, static discharger; G, rudder hinge access; H, hinge; J, fin-cap edge; K, "take care ! honeycomb"; L, rudder power units, working fluid SA18, 5000DA, AMG 10.

4

The Interceptors

IT IS PERHAPS preferable to call these versions "fighters", if only because an estimated 1,800 are operational in the regiments of the FA (*frontovaya aviatsiya*, frontal aviation, meaning the vast tactical air forces which support the ground forces) and only a little over 400 in the IA-PVO (fighter aviation of the dedicated air-defence forces, which is an entirely separate branch of the armed forces). The IA-PVO is equipped with large all-weather interceptors able to kill at a distance, and demanding long paved runways and large ground facilities and staff. The FA is equipped with tough battleworthy aircraft able to operate from rough, austerely equipped forward bases without paved runways or taxiways. It so happens that the MiG-23 fighter versions can meet the needs of both operators, and this automatically made it attractive to many export customers.

Known fighter versions

To begin by running quickly through the known fighter versions, the initial Lyul'ka-powered aircraft was covered in section 2. The first true series version was the MiG-23M, called Flogger-B by NATO. Usually the suffix letter M means *Modifikatsirovanni*, or modified. In this case the modification was very extensive, caused by switching to the R-27 engine. This model also introduced full combat equipment, and introduced many other details to assist front-line maintenance. It was followed in 1973 by the MiG-23MF, F meaning *forsirovanni* or boosted, which in turn signifies an increase in propulsive thrust. This was achieved by switching to the R-29 engine. The MF also introduced a new radar and much other new equipment, but as this did not greatly affect the external appearance the NATO name stayed Flogger-B. Next came an export version, described in the last chapter. Last of the fighter variants known in the West is a slightly modified MF which visited Finland and France in 1978. As it has a smaller

dorsal fin this did receive a new NATO designation, Flogger-G, but there were other significant changes in this version as described later.

Highest military aircraft output

It is rather remarkable that no significant new version has appeared in 13 years since the current engine was introduced. The Soviet Union is loath to disrupt high-rate production lines, and output of all fighter and attack versions combined has been running at about 400 per year for more than ten years, easily exceeding the deliveries of any other military aeroplane in the world over this period. The only possible conclusion must be that the original aircraft was judged adequate for the job and still meets the requirements with only minor updating. All the indications are that both fighter and attack versions will continue in front-line service into the 1990s alongside the next-generation MiG-29 and Su-27. On the other hand it is interesting to note that, while India—which had a great influence on the MiG-21 programme and had built up a very close working relationship with both the Soviet Ministry of Aviation Production and the MiG OKB—not only bought a large number of the attack version but also bought a manufacturing licence, it did not purchase a single example of the MiG-23 fighter versions.

Similarities to Phantom

To a first approximation, the MiG-23 is rather like a Soviet equivalent of the F-4 Phantom. It has roughly the same level of technology, roughly the same capabilities as a fighter, and a generally similar level of performance. It gains tremendously from having the variable-sweep wing, which enables it to reconcile good dash performance with good short-field performance. This tends to make it smaller, and further gains result from having only one engine and one seat. No meaningful prices for the Soviet aircraft have been published, but early versions probably cost about half as much as Phantoms built at the same time.

"Look-down . . . " capability

Little appears to be known about the equipment of the pre-production and MiG-23M versions, and it was not until the upgraded MF that the US Department of Defense published its assessment, "The first Soviet aircraft with a demonstrated ability to track and engage targets flying below its own altitude". Even this falls short of so-called "look down, shoot down" capability, which implies the ability to intercept targets flying only just above the ground. This is a demanding requirement, calling for specially designed radar and missiles, unless the fighter is able to acquire the target visually and close the range sufficiently for it to use IR-homing missiles or a gun.

Amazingly, the correct designation of the MF radar appears not to be known in the West. To NATO it is High Lark, and it is clearly broadly comparable to the Westinghouse AWG-10 used in some Phantoms, both in bulk and operating modes. It has a mechanically steered scanner of about 0.8m (32in) diameter, housed within a large radome moulded mainly in glassfibre and carrying a short pitot/static tube on the end. Insertion of an object of this nature, opaque to radar signals, inevitably degrades and slightly distorts the outgoing and incoming signals, and it is especially surprising in view of the addition of a large pitot head on the upper right side of the nose. High Lark is a pulse doppler set, one of the first in production in the Soviet Union, in which both pulses and the doppler shift in wavelength of the reflected signals are used together. The doppler shift depends on the relative velocity between the radar and its target. Thus, a vehicle will show up as having a different doppler shift from the

Below: A MiG-23MF Flogger-G visiting the Ilmavoimat (Finnish air force) Karelian Wing in August 1978. Apart from the centre-line tank there are no stores or pylons. Note the part-open canopy.

unmoving road, and a speeding enemy aircraft will show up clearly against the ground or sea. Liquid cooled High Lark operates in J-waveband, at frequencies between 10-20GHz, and detects typical airborne targets at 85km (53 miles), tracking them from 55km (34 miles) or less.

Infra-red receiver

Under the forward fuselage, so close to the nose gear that the rear part of its fairing is half on one nose-gear door and half on the other, is a box housing a sensor which looks ahead through left and right "chisel" windows, which are inclined back in both plan and side elevation. Early Western assessments almost always described this as a "laser ranger", but such a device would have little value to an air-combat fighter. Despite its external similarity to a laser the author has no doubt that it must be the 26-SH1 IR (infra-red) receiver, able to detect the faint heat from hostile aircraft at a distance of tens of kilometres and, by a direct analog link, tell the IR seeker heads of selected missiles exactly where to look in order to acquire the target. On the ground the windows of this small gondola are covered with a protective shield carrying the aircraft's individual number, usually painted white on a red background.

Above: It is practice to leave the canopy open when taxiing. Note the q-feel pitot, Odd Rods IFF aerial, temperature probe, rear-view mirror and, under "28", the puzzling blister.

The Flogger-Gs which visited Finland and France in 1978 had this sensor removed; instead, the underside of the nose was bulged immediately ahead of the nosewheel bay as if the twin doors had to clear some internal projection (taken care of on the majority of MFs by the sensor fairings).

Apart from using the radar in its ground-map mode the chief navaid is a doppler radar, which gives precise groundspeed and drift, in other words the velocity relative to the Earth's surface. This has a quad aerial array in the underside of the nose covered by a dielectric panel forming the underskin between the main radar and the IR sensor. On the Flogger-Gs which visited the West the circular aerial apertures were visible but set into metal skin, the large (usually black) radome being absent. Another and equally unexplained difference was that the forward-sector ILS aerial, looking like a small metal crossbow, was moved from its usual position on the left under the doppler radome to the corresponding location on the right. (One British report stated that it was the doppler that was moved, and added that the bulged nosegear bay was because of use of a different leg without levered suspension; the photos

Above: A MiG-23MF Flogger-B making a cold (non-afterburning) takeoff. The ventral fin swings down before the main gears are fully retracted. Note the long dorsal fin.

show both conclusions to be erroneous.)

Small details abound round the nose. The upper right pitot has been mentioned. On the centreline in front of the windscreen is the SRO-2M (NATO Odd Rods) IFF installation covering the forward and upper sectors, via the group of three (short, medium and long) vertical rod aerials. The fighter versions have no IFF covering the underside and rear, and

Below: A detail of the underside of a MiG-23MF showing the two large Reper-M electronic-warfare aerials on each side of the underfin, covering the lower hemisphere.

increasingly Soviet tactical aircraft are managing with just a single aerial installation. About 0.4m (16in) further forward is a freely pivoted yaw vane. This is a simple weathercock which serves any sideslip and feeds corrective signals into the weapon-aiming subsystem. Even more important is the corresponding weathercock sensor working in the vertical plane, pivoted about a horizontal axis on the left side of the forward fuselage. This measures AOA (angle of attack), and is used not only to feed data to the weapon-aiming subsystem but also as a primary aid to accurate flight, especially during the landing approach.

Inlets for cooling avionics

Low on each side of the nose, immediately behind the radome, is a ram air inlet for cooling the high-power avionics bays. The avionics boxes are racked on lower and upper levels, and each cooling air inlet is bifurcated to duct air to both levels. Hot air is ducted overboard or, if needed, to heat the cockpit. Near the windshield on the left is one of three small air-data sensors, the others being under the flanks of the inlet ducts. From their appearance these are venturis incorporating a thermistor-type temperature sensor, but it is easy to guess wrongly. Each is an open cylindrical tube standing 130mm (5in) away from the fuselage. Low on the left side of the nose, near the nose leg, is a long but quite slim blister whose purpose is unknown beyond the fact that it is an avionic item and certainly not a pipe fairing.

As noted earlier the canopy is relatively small, the design being biased in favour of rear protection and low drag at the expense of poor rear view. The latter is provided mainly by the rear-view mirror, which is larger than that of late MiG-21s and mounted in a longitudinal frame along the upper centreline. The canopy hinges up from the rear under the thrust of a hydraulic jack ahead of the hinge, and the aircraft is taxied with the canopy slightly open. The cockpit itself is described in a separate box. Immediately to the rear is the flush ADF sense aerial in the upper skin of the dorsal spine, which in this aircraft is of modest size and tapers away as the tail is reached. On each side of the spine below the ADF are hot air and gas outlets, one being from an air-cycle machine in

Below: Typically simple and tough, yet in many ways a very advanced engine, the R-29B is one of the most powerful in service in the world. This tail-on detail shows: A, fairing over nylon cord pulling drag-chute doors tightly together; B, translating nozzle actuation ring; C, 18-petal primary nozzle; D, blunt rear end to fixed taileron root; E, perforated and coated afterburner liner; F, three flameholder gutters; G, airbrake jack; H, 18-petal secondary nozzle; J, drain mast; K, underfin.

Left: The fully garbed pilot of a MiG-23MF fighter of the VVS (Soviet air force) Frontal Aviation. This particular aircraft is a sub-type whose canopy has a strong axial frame along the top incorporating the rear-view mirror. Some MiG-23s have two extra mirrors fixed to the canopy front frame.

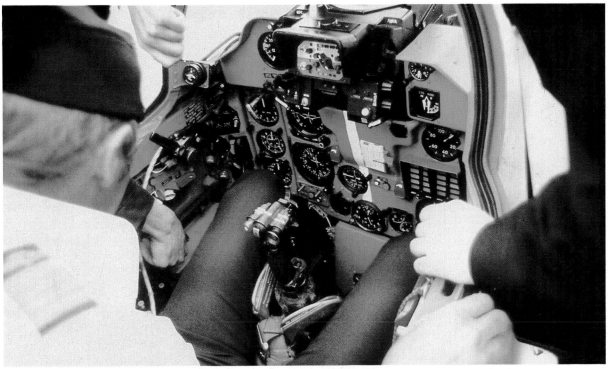

Above: The cockpit of a MiG-23BN Flogger-F, with a visiting Swedish pilot in the ejection seat. The panel is uncluttered, even though there is not one electronic display. At top centre is the head-up weapon-aiming sight, with its own control panel. Note the profusion of controls on top of the stick.

Right: A remarkably fine photograph, taken with "fisheye" wide angle lens, of a Flogger-G pilot with his two wingmen. This particular series of aircraft have the canopy divided into left/right halves by an axial frame long the top. Note the engine air inlets just visible on each side astern.

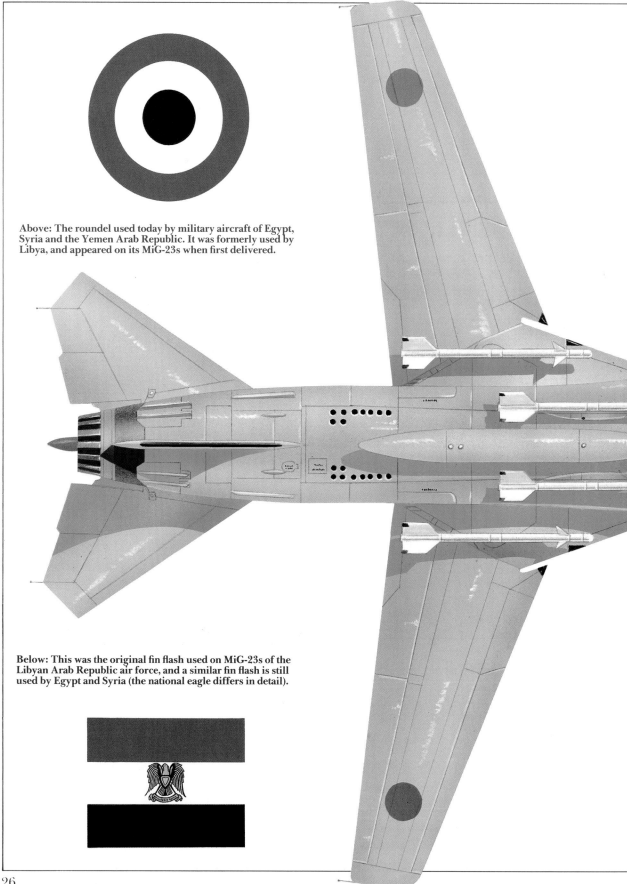

Above: The roundel used today by military aircraft of Egypt, Syria and the Yemen Arab Republic. It was formerly used by Libya, and appeared on its MiG-23s when first delivered.

Below: This was the original fin flash used on MiG-23s of the Libyan Arab Republic air force, and a similar fin flash is still used by Egypt and Syria (the national eagle differs in detail).

Below: Plan view from above of a MiG-23MF Flogger-E of the Libyan Arab Republic air force, in the current plain green national insignia. The pivoting wings are set at 45°, which brings the leading-edge dogteeth well away from the fixed glove. Some Libyan aircraft are now pale grey overall.

Above left: Plan view from below of the same Libyan MiG-23MF Flogger-E. The wings are shown at the minimum sweep angle of 16°, which brings the leading-edge dogteeth close to the fixed glove, creating a slot effect. Missiles are K-13As (AA-2 Atolls), a copy of the AIM-9B Sidewinder. Note tabbed tailerons.

Below: Side elevation of the same aircraft, which was intercepted over the Gulf of Sirte by US Navy fighters six years ago. The usual Libyan practice is to number the aircraft in Arabic on the left and in Western numerals on the right. Note the small Jay Bird radar, also used on the two-seat trainer version.

Above: The badge of excellence awarded on a unit basis to fighter regiments of the VVS (Soviet air force) Frontal Aviation. Formerly called Guards, they are now called Red Banner units.

Below: Plan view of the early MiG-23MF Flogger-B shown in the other views, with wings fully swept to 72°. At that time (1975) the trailing edges of the tailerons (tailplanes) were straight.

Right: In the head-on view the completely flat vertical sides of the engine inlets can be seen (on the MiG-27 these edges are bulged outward). Note the usual nose-up ground attitude.

Below: A Frontal Aviation MiG-23MF Flogger-E on display at Kubinka for Swedish air force visitors. The representative weapons included Atoll and Advanced Atoll AAMs.

Right: Side elevation of one of the first production MiG-23MF Flogger-B interceptors of Soviet Frontal Aviation, shown with wings at maximum sweep of 72°. Many small details differ from aircraft of the same basic type now being delivered.

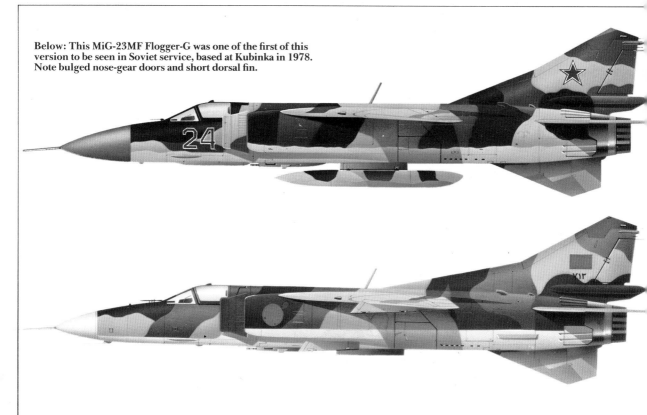

Below: This MiG-23MF Flogger-G was one of the first of this version to be seen in Soviet service, based at Kubinka in 1978. Note bulged nose-gear doors and short dorsal fin.

Above: Another Libyan MiG-23MF Flogger-E seen in 1980. This shows Arabic numbering on the left, in this case 712. These export models with the Jay Bird radar have the ILS aerial moved forward nearer the nose. Several were destroyed, including four at Benina, in the US attack on 14 April 1986.

Right: Plan views showing the top and bottom of the left half of a standard MiG-27 Flogger-D. Distinguished by its simple engine inlets, this also has a bulged main-gear bay, six-barrel gun and pylons wide apart under the inlet ducts. The rest is similar to the MiG-23BN Flogger-F and -H.

Left: A MiG-23BN hybrid attack version presented for inspection at Kubinka, near Moscow, by a visiting Swedish air force team. Sixteen FAB-250 bombs are loaded, plus two of a different kind of store on the rear-fuselage side pylons.

Below: Side elevation of a MiG-23MF Flogger-B of recent construction, contrasting with the drawing on the previous pages. Missiles are R-23R (AA-7 Apex radar version) under the wings and R-60 (AA-8 Aphid), the small dogfight missiles on the fuselage pylons.

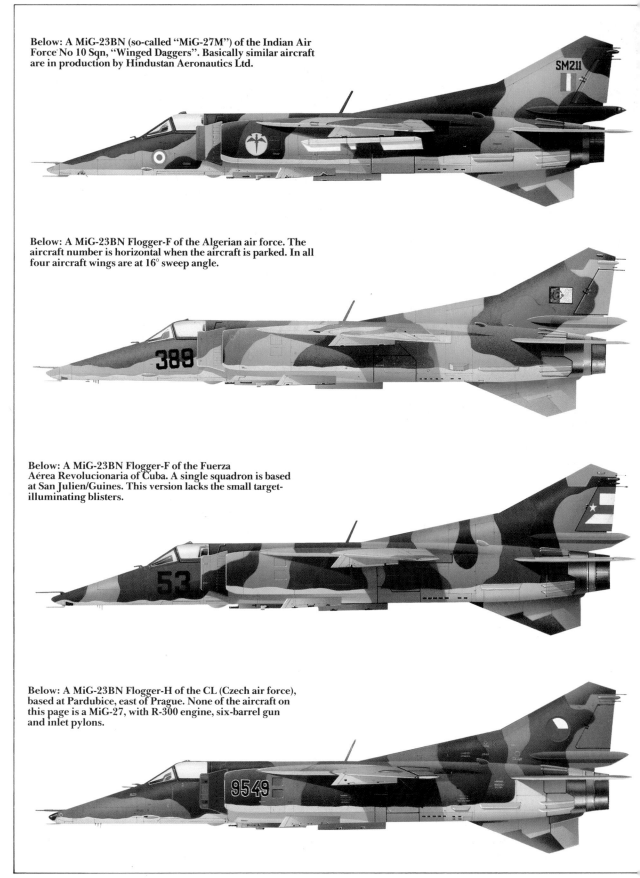

Below: A MiG-23BN (so-called "MiG-27M") of the Indian Air Force No 10 Sqn, "Winged Daggers". Basically similar aircraft are in production by Hindustan Aeronautics Ltd.

Below: A MiG-23BN Flogger-F of the Algerian air force. The aircraft number is horizontal when the aircraft is parked. In all four aircraft wings are at 16° sweep angle.

Below: A MiG-23BN Flogger-F of the Fuerza Aérea Revolucionaria of Cuba. A single squadron is based at San Julien/Guines. This version lacks the small target-illuminating blisters.

Below: A MiG-23BN Flogger-H of the CL (Czech air force), based at Pardubice, east of Prague. None of the aircraft on this page is a MiG-27, with R-300 engine, six-barrel gun and inlet pylons.

Above: Cis-Carpathian Military District exercises in August 1984. The MiG-23MF Flogger-B shows: A, fairing (fuel pipe ?); B, actuator cover plates on outer two LE flaps; C, notched tip of aileron; D, open ventral doors, E, pipe fairing (like A, not on Flogger-G); F, trim access; G, "warning, honeycomb".

the ECS (environmental control system). Close alongside are the boundary-layer channels, and the bleed duct exits above and below the main inlets. Further aft, on the centreline, is the VHF communications aerial in the form of a raked rigid blade.

The engine installation has already been described, but further detail on the fighter propulsion system may be useful. Attention focusses on the flat, vertical inner wall of the inlet. This begins with a fixed leading edge machined from solid metal and leading to a section covered with spots which are flush rivets attaching the skin to the closely spaced inner structure. This terminates in a vertical piano hinge to which is attached the forward inlet ramp.

This is perforated by holes through which is sucked the potentially sluggish or turbulent boundary-layer air, and an accompanying sketch shows the arrangement of these holes. At the rear end of this panel is the piano hinge joining it to the second movable panel downstream, and on the inner side of this hinge is the vertical actuator which, via bellcranks at top and bottom, moves the hinge in and out. The inlet throat is wide open on takeoff and at low speeds, and fully restricted at Mach 2. The geometry is extremely like that of the F-4 Phantom II.

In the right main-gear bay is a screwed on inspection hatch giving a view of the front of the engine. Above the rear fuselage are two projecting cooling-air inlets which discharge through the annular space between the secondary and primary nozzles. The latter can be seen in a close-up photo taken from the rear, which also shows detail of one of the four airbrakes. In normal operation all four airbrakes are opened and closed in unison, and the author has no information on why, or how, this one was left open on this occasion. On many MFs the engine-bay drain mast is the first thing to hit the ground in an abnormally nose-high takeoff, and on later aircraft it is shorter (in some it appears to be absent). Under the rear fuselage, on each side of the underfin leading edge, is a prominent projection with a flat horizontal underside containing a white disc about 0.16m (6.7in) in diameter. They are stencilled "antenna REPER-M", but the author does not know what this means (RE would be "radio-elektrichyeskii"). These look like RWR receivers, but it would be unreasonable to have two of them facing straight downwards, and for these to be absent from the dedicated attack version. Close to the left-hand installation are two small doors in tandem, the front one roughly square and the rear one rounded. These are opened against the airstream whenever the landing gear is extended.

A little higher up on each side, ahead of the lower airbrakes, are parallel-sided fairings, and similar but shorter fairings are seen on top of the fuselage on each side near the leading edge of the giant dorsal fin. The author believes these to be fuel pipes enabling fuel to flow between tanks separated by major fuselage frames. But the interesting thing is that these fairings are absent from the MiG-23MF variant known as Flogger-G which has visited the West. The main distinguishing feature of this version is its fin (vertical stabilizer), whose leading edge is almost straight instead of being kinked forwards in a giant dorsal fin. The aircraft that came to Finland and France also lacked pylons and the undernose sensor. The type was dismissed by Western analysts as a special stripped-down display variant, until it was realized it is a regular production machine. It is said to have "lighter radar", and this would go well with elimination of a rear-fuselage tank and reduction in fin size, though there would inevitably be a reduction in range. Current FA aircraft of this type have a new undernose sensor of smaller cross-section, with three triangular front windows meeting at a point.

Standard inbuilt armament comprises a GSh-23L twin-barrel gun. The gun installation itself is similar to that in MiG-21s, but in the MiG-23 there is no problem with the ammunition which is fed from a simple box above the gun. Despite the proximity of

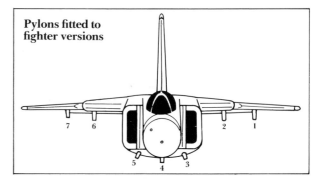

Above: External stores stations of a MiG-23: 1 and 7, fixed pylons for ferry tanks at 16° sweep only; 2 and 6, R-23R (Apex), twin R-60 (Aphid) or AA-2 or 2-2 Atoll; 3 and 5, single or twin Aphid or Atoll, or various other stores; 4, 800lit tank or (reportedly) various ground-attack stores.

the two muzzles, firing the gun has no adverse effect on the engine. Other weapons are hung on the seven pylons. Nos 1, 4 and 7 are plumbed for tanks and have never been seen carrying anything else. Other loads are as outlined in a diagram, and there are no pylons on the rear fuselage. The big R-23 missiles give a useful stand-off kill capability, and one can assume that both R-23T (IR) and R-23R (radar) versions have capability against low-flying targets. The smaller K-13A (AA-2 Atoll) and longer AA-2-2 Advanced Atoll are derivatives of early Sidewinders, while the R-60 (AA-8 Aphid) is a highly manoeuvrable dogfight weapon intended as the next-generation replacement.

Early descriptions of the MiG-23 fighter described it as having a secondary ground-attack role. There is no obvious reason why this should not be so, but the author has never seen surface-attack stores hung on one of these aircraft and MiG-23 pilots have denied having ground-attack tasks or training.

This completes the outline of the fighter versions. It must be said however, that the Flogger-G has been widely reported as the MiG-23bis. This may well be so, but the author has no evidence for the following allegations concerning this aircraft which have often appeared since 1984: it has much greater (2400lit, 525gal) fuel capacity than earlier versions (evidence suggests it has less), a completely new radar with full look-down capability and presenting its information on a HUD instead of a traditional HDD, a new nose gear with larger tyres, and "mainwheel legs like those of the MiG-27 providing ground clearance for an 800lit tank on the centreline". All MiG-23s can carry a tank of this size.

5
Attack Versions

A VERY powerful engine, swing wings and excellent rough-field landing gear give all members of the Ye-23 family considerable flexibility to fly all kinds of tactical air-combat, strike and reconnaissance missions. At the very start of the project the decision was taken to forgo this capability, and instead to build dedicated fighter versions and attack versions. This was a decision of uncommon interest. After all, the basic Ye-23 was designed as a bi-sonic missile-armed all-weather fighter. Such an aircraft does not form the ideal basis for a dedicated attack aircraft, and the latter—hardly if ever supersonic—certainly does not need an airframe designed for over Mach 2.

At least one Western writer has reported that the original attack version was the MiG-23BN (Flogger-F), which differs from the fighter only in its forward fuselage and its tyre sizes, this later being followed by a "more extensive revision" with a different engine installation. To show how difficult it is to guess correctly where the Soviet Union is concerned, what actually happened was the other way round. The original attack aircraft was a major redesign specifically for this role; only later was an attack vesion produced with the original (Mach 2) engine installation. Why this should have been done remains a mystery.

There was no publicity for any early prototype of the attack variant, which instead suddenly appeared in service with the GSFG (Group of Soviet Forces in Germany) in 1975. Curiously, it was designated MiG-27; what was curious was that, traditionally, odd type numbers were reserved for fighters, whereas

Below: Head-on view of the alleged "MiG-27M" which, as explained on p.47, is clearly not a MiG-27 of any sort. A ground cover is fitted over the forward-looking laser ranger.

Above: An early MiG-27 on its landing approach in East Germany in 1975. Shadows cast by the low Sun emphasize the depressed flaps along leading and trailing edges of the 16° wing.

this aircraft was specifically for ground attack. NATO called it Flogger-D.

As far as one can tell, most of the airframe is identical with the fighter, and spare parts can probably be built into either. The chief differences are to be found in the forward fuselage, ahead of a modified inclined aft pressure bulkhead. In front of this virtually everything is changed. To improve pilot view the seat is raised, the canopy redesigned with greater depth and without an upper longitudinal frame, and the windscreen assembly made much deeper and sloped downwards, and restressed for severe birdstrikes. The much better view down and ahead is retained by redesigning the nose to be much shorter and wedge-shaped, sloping sharply down to a pointed tip (Soviet nickname is *utkanoz*, duck nose).

The multimode radar is, of course, eliminated. In its place is an LRMTS (laser ranger and marked-target seeker) similar to that of the RAF Jaguar, aft of which are both a terrain-avoidance radar and a doppler navigation radar (different from that used in the fighters, if the radome is any guide), with the usual ILS aerial mounted below on the centreline. Further aft, in the position occupied by the IR sensor in the fighter, is a radar altimeter. Altogether this

adds up to an excellent package for daytime low-level navigation and weapon delivery. The much reduced nose moment-arm (component weights multiplied by distances from the aircraft centre of gravity) was restored by adding slabs of thick titanium armour on each side of the cockpit, and also below and at front and rear, the side panels being the largest and thickest. These are scabbed on externally, with bevelled edges, drag being of little importance. The aircraft number is painted on them in most user air forces. The engine was changed for a different species of R-29, designated R-29-300 with a simpler afterburner and nozzle matched to subsonic Mach numbers. This slightly reduces thrust ratings in afterburner, though dry ratings are almost unchanged, as is the engine itself. Objectives were to reduce installed engine weight and cost, and to minimize fuel consumption in subsonic cruise. The nozzle has much shorter petals which make no attempt to achieve the optimum convergent/divergent bellmouth profile for peak thrust at Mach 2. Early Western reports stated that the nozzle had just two settings, open and closed, but this statement was accompanied by so many gross errors concerning the engine that it cannot be relied upon. The basic engine upstream of the afterburner is broadly similar to that of the fighter.

Inlets not variable geometry

The policy of simplification naturally also extends to the air inlets. These have a slightly greater cross-section area and profile than those of the fighter at takeoff, and there is no variable geometry. The increase in inlet area results from a slight outward bulge in the outer lip of the inlet, that of the fighter being a vertical straight line. The inner wall stands away from the fuselage by the same distance as in the fighter, but in side elevation it is much smaller, extending only a few inches ahead of the inlet and not at all above and below. Thus, the entire rear edge of the side armour aft of the cockpit can be seen, and the most obvious recognition feature is that there are no large aft-facing exits above and below the inlet, for the withdrawal of boundary-layer airflow. Less obvious is the omission of the alternative boundary-layer overboard exit through grills in the external skin above and below the duct. The much more severe birdstrike problem with the MiG-27 was rec-

ognized from the start, but all recent Tumanskii turbojets have robust first-stage blades and little needed to be done to either the engine or inlets to meet qualification requirements.

To recapitulate, the basic engine of the MiG-27 is essentially the same as that of the fighter. There have been several Western reports suggesting that it is in some way a totally different engine of much reduced power, quite apart from the afterburning ratings. For example the April 1986 *Air International* gives ratings of 6,500kg (14,330lb) dry and 8,130kg (17,920lb) with full afterburner. The author can only comment that as these ratings came from a Soviet brochure prepared for India, which country has quoted them ever since, the Soviet designers have found some new laws of physics. You do not enlarge the inlets and open up the nozzle and then reduce thrust by 35 per cent! Common sense should show that the MiG-27, which takes off at generally much higher weights than the fighter, needs a similar level of thrust. Put another way, there is no way the thrust of the basic turbojet (ignoring afterburner) could have been reduced from 8,000kg (17,637lb) to 6,500kg without restricting it to a ridiculously low rpm and turbine gas temperature.

Indeed, the basic demand for operation from short front-line airstrips ideally demands more engine power and not less, though the final propulsion system is a compromise dictated by the factors listed earlier. To get airborne at high weights from such bases it was at first thought that the MiG-27 used a.t.o. (assisted takeoff) rockets, and Western analysts lost little time in pointing out the "mountings" for these on the sides of the rear fuselage. Not until ten years later was it realized this was a mistake, and the correct explanation is given later.

Bigger wheels and tyres

On the other hand, the need to operate from rough unpaved surfaced did call for much lower tyre pressures, and the only way this can be reconciled with increased weights is to use bigger tyres. In the case of the nose gear there was an overriding limitation on available width when retracted, so the only answer was to increase the diameter of the wheels and tyres. Nobody in the West appears to have taken the trouble to read the tyre sizes, but the enlargement is enough for bulges to be needed in the bay doors. Rather surprisingly, whereas the fighter's nosewheels are shielded by a wraparound mudguard, the larger wheels of the MiG-27 are fitted with a smaller mudguard unit which does not extend around the outer sides. According to a Czech officer rough-field operations can result in splattering of the underside of the aircraft, but "we can clean it up again quickly". It is possible the fighter nose gear might have been prone to clogging with mud and/or snow, but this is speculation.

Centre fuselage bulge

In the case of the main gear the only possible answer was to enlarge the wheels and tyres, even though there was no spare room in the bay. Choosing the lesser of two evils, the diameter was unchanged but the width increased considerably (author's estimate, 100mm, 4in). Again, somebody might like to read off the tyre size when they have a moment. In this case the bulge was not just a mere blister over the retracted wheel but a complete structural redesign of the centre fuselage. In both side and plan view the bulge is quite pronounced, and though it does not disrupt streamline airflow it looks contrary to arearule design precepts, which call for the body cross-section to be not bulged but waisted alongside the wing in high-speed flight. Area rule is important at Mach numbers over about 0.8, where the wing would be swept back, making the position of the bulge more adverse.

Predictably, there was also major revision of the air-data and EW (electronic warfare) systems. Repeatedly, the Soviet Union has shown itself willing to start again "from square one" to ensure an uncompromised result, even when something 95 per cent as good already existed. Thus, the air-data system of the MiG-27 features a large probe, quite different from that of the fighter, located on the upper left side of the nose. The small ram probe (a temperature thermistor according to most accounts) on the left of the windscreen is duplicated, the fighter having only one. The AOA wind vane on the left side of the forward fuselage is unaltered, as is the group of aerials at the top of the fin and the VHF aerial above the fuselage. The SRO-2M IFF, however, is relocated on the underside of the nose, and the Reper-M aerials in the underside of the rear fuselage are replaced by attachments which can be used for bombs or for chaff/flare cartridge dispensers (these are the items at first called "rocket attachments").

Sensor and aerial fairings

A completely new feature is the addition of a bullet-shaped fairing projecting ahead from the mid-point of each wing glove, in line with the glove pylon. That on the left is an EO (electro-optical) sensor, with a circular aperture about 100mm (4in) in diameter. That on the right has been surmised as a missile-guidance aerial, and this may well be right because with the glove and outer-wing Sirena 3 receivers there is no need for any further passive receiver looking ahead.

Armament is naturally very different from the fighter. The GSh-23L gun is replaced by a six-barrel

Below: Another from the first MiG-27 (Flogger-D) regiment to be despatched to East Germany in 1975. The short "ducknose" is obvious, but it took time for Western analysts to identify the numerous other new features. Not apparent from this side elevation are the wide tyres on the mainwheels.

Above: Still the best photograph of the sensors of an early MiG-27, even if a familiar one, this also highlights the bulkier mainwheels. It also emphasizes the flattened triangular cross-section of the down-sloping ducknose, the scabbed-on side armour and the widely separated pylons under the engine air ducts.

weapon superficially similar to the American M61, but of 23mm calibre. The gun is installed almost wholly externally, which at the cost of increased drag eliminates gun-gas accretion problems. The muzzles are immediately aft of the nose-gear bay, the barrel at 6 o'clock being the one that fires. The nine stores hardpoints are slightly different from those of the fighter, and the two forward fuselage stations are moved from the fuselage proper to a new location well outboard under the inlet ducts. All stations are restressed for much greater weights than for the fighter. Typical loads are given in an accompanying diagram.

Export Flogger puzzles

Curiously, the basic MiG-27, called Flogger-D by NATO, has seldom been exported. Even more strangely, the corresponding export aircraft, sold to (at least) Algeria, Cuba, Egypt (formerly), Ethiopia, Iraq, Libya, Syria and Vietnam, is the MiG-23BN (Flogger-F), which has almost the same engine, inlets, nozzle and gun as the fighters. Such an aircraft must be considerably more expensive than the MiG-27, would gain nothing in attack capability, and still have

little air-combat capability. Yet a further puzzle is that, though the 23BN has variable-geometry inlets, the small venturi pressure sensors under the inlets of the fighter, and said to control the variable-geometry system, are absent!

Dating from about 1978, the next version to be identified was another hybrid MiG-23BN, called Flogger-H, which resembles the previous BN except for the addition of a dielectric blister low down on each side of the nose, just ahead of the nose gear. This has been described as a target-illuminating radar, though it has not been explained why there are two such blisters. As before, nobody appears to have taken the trouble to read the descriptive stencilling, despite the public exhibition of such aircraft as supplied to India (see final chapter).

Varying equipment standards

Some MiG-23BN sub-types clearly have a relatively low equipment level, lacking the EO and ASM-guidance pods on the wing gloves. Others, including those for India, not only have the missile guidance pod on the right glove (and relocated below the wing, terminating almost in contact with the pylon) but they also have a completely new and large dielectric area in the adjacent leading edge, with a corresponding panel in the left glove. Thus, there are three leading-edge aerials in the left wing and four in the right, as shown in a diagram photograph on page 47 of an Indian BN.

Chronologically the ultimate attack version is another MiG-27, not the same as the MIG-27M

Below: Weapon stations of the MiG-27, for comparison with those of the MiG-23 family on p.34: 1 and 9, fixed removable pylons for ferry tanks at 16° only; 2 and 8, 1,000kg rated for wide range of stores; 3 and 7, rear-fuselage pylons for bombs or dispensers; 4 and 6, 1,000kg multi-use pylons; 5, 800 lit tank.

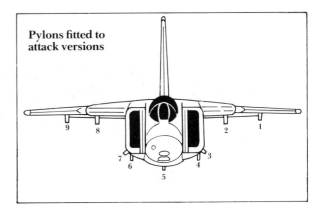

Pylons fitted to attack versions

going into production in India, and called by NATO Flogger-J. This has a major upgrade in navigation and weapon-aiming systems, though the changes appear not to have been analysed in the West. Features of the nose include blade aerials on the underside, a chin blister which almost certainly houses terrain-following (or improved terrain-avoidance) radar, a lip above the nose (which could be several things) and three minor changes. The big air-data boom is usually absent, as are any sensor fairings on the wing gloves, but most aircraft of this type have small underfins on each side of the muzzles of the six-barrel gun. These are clearly to reduce blast disturbance to the engine inlet airflow. An important airframe modification is a small leading-edge root extension which runs parallel to the centre-line until near the top of the inlet, when it cuts diagonally inwards. Such root extensions have an effect on gross lift and aerodynamic pitching moment much greater than their small area might suggest, especially at high angles of attack, because they not only give lift in their own right but also create vortices which improve attached flow over the glove and top of the fuselage. Somewhat similar extensions are seen on the wings and fins of the MiG-31, these being absent from the predecessor MiG-25.

The author has never seen an attack variant that did not have the parallel-sided fairings on the sides of the rear fuselage and above the fuselage on each side of the leading edge of the dorsal fin, apparently betokening the increased internal fuel capacity. All recent production, of both the MiG-27 and MiG-23BN sub-series, have the extended-chord inboard tailerons, resulting in a kinked trailing edge.

Many unknown factors

As in the case of other members of the Flogger family, there are still plenty of things we do not yet know about the attack variants. Even the sensor kit in the nose remains largely a matter of guesswork, despite the fact that stencilling on the MiG-23BNs supplied to the Indian Air Force is all in English! The improved suite fitted to the Flogger-J, which is now generally believed to be the 27M, is even more of an enigma, as all photographs so far released are of exceptionally poor quality, and the clearer one was heavily retouched before being issued.

What is beyond dispute is that these aircraft are extremely potent and formidable, and relative to their counterparts elsewhere are superior to the fighter versions. Not many illustrations exist of the wealth of ordnance available to Soviet Frontal Avia-

Below: The latest illustration to become available of a MiG-27, showing a semi-active laser-homing air-to-surface missile (almost certainly the type known to NATO as AS-X-14 but not yet given a published code-name) and what has been described as a GSh-23L gun pod well aft on the fuselage centreline.

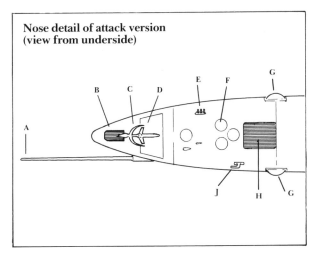

Nose detail of attack version (view from underside)

Above: Underside view of the nose of a typical MiG-27 Flogger-D showing locations of some of the sensors, about which there is still uncertainty: A, air-data probe; B, laser ranger; C, ILS aerial; D, main doppler radar; E, IFF aerial; F, two of these are glass windows; G, target illuminations; H, radar altimeter.

tion, but it includes more than 200 types of bomb of which virtually all can be carried by these aircraft. The rear-fuselage pylons are unusual, and while they obviously cause no unacceptable in-flight instability they must result in a noticeable nose-down pitching moment when these bombs are released. Practically

Below: Another modern Flogger-J, in a picture released in the West in 1986, the official caption stating that it is carrying a laser-guided bomb. Such weapons are widely used by MiG-27 regiments, but the author's eyesight has failed to identify one here. Note rear-fuselage chaff/flare dispenser.

nothing is known about the available ECM jammer pods and cluster weapons, and even the ASMs (air-to-surface missiles) are known only as vague external shapes. The weapon called AS-7 Kerry has been in use for over a decade. The AS-10 has not been seen but is thought to be slightly smaller, and its laser guidance may give it a nose resembling Paveway and similar LGBs (laser-guided bombs) in the West. We have a single photograph of a MiG-27M carrying the considerably larger AS-14, which has the same configuration as AS-7 but very much larger canards and tailfins.

New, faster-firing gun

This photograph also shows what appears to be the gun pod on the rear centreline pylon. These pods have been described in the West as containing guns with "barrels that can be depressed for attacking ground targets". It is not possible to hinge barrels separately from the breech, as a little thought will show! The complete gun must clearly be arranged to pivot, the angle being about 18°. The gun is probably of 23mm calibre, but has a single barrel. It is a new model, lighter and faster-firing than the NR-23 and similar guns (used, for example, in bomber turrets). The left and right guns may be toed inwards to assist in firing along a single ground track, such as a hostile column moving along a road.

6
Trainers

FOR MANY years it has been Soviet policy to produce dual-control two-pilot versions of all single-seat combat aircraft. In the case of some recent types the two-seater has not yet been identified—examples are the Su-25 and MiG-29—but the MiG-23 was designed in parallel with a two-pilot version which entered VVS service only a short time after the MiG-23M single-seater. Rather remarkably, the progressive developments and changes made to the various single-seaters do not appear to have been applied to the two-seat version. All of the latter that have so far been seen appear outwardly to be almost the same as the first.

The MiG-23U (U for *Uchyebnii*, trainer) is used both for conversion to the type and for weapons training, though the latter extends only to simple attacks with guns, rockets and possibly practice bombs using visual sighting. It is extremely unlikely that the trainers figure in the Frontal Aviation operational inventory.

Similarities to production fighter

Predictably, the MiG-23U is a minimum-change aircraft, the basic airframe and R-27 engine being identical to the initial production fighter, the MiG-23M. Thus, the inlets and nozzle are designed for flight at high supersonic Mach numbers, and according to brochures the performance of the trainer is "the same as that of the single-seat versions".

Nevertheless, a second seat could not be fitted into a MiG-23 without forcing relocation of the inter-duct equipment items, most of which are electronics. Some of these were moved to the nose, resulting in replacement of the powerful radar by a small low-power set which is universally assumed to be the same as the radar known to NATO as Jay Bird, fitted to later production blocks of MiG-21. This opens up almost 1m (39in) of additional nose space, and this took care of most of the routine "black boxes".

Several Western writers have stated as a fact that the MiG-23U has less internal fuel than the fighters—for example, *Air International's* wording is "at some significant expense in internal fuel"—but in the author's opinion the difference is not significant. It will be noted that the MiG-23U does possess the parallel-sided fairing on each side of the rear fuselage (but not alongside the tip of the dorsal fin) which probably means additional fuel in the rear fuselage.

Tandem-cockpit arrangement

When the MiG-23U was designed the MiG OKB was very experienced with providing backseat instructors with roof periscopes. It had no experience with the modern style of tandem-cockpit trainer in which the back seat is positioned 0.4m (16in) or so higher than the front. Today this staggered arrangement is adopted without question, but in the MiG-23U the instructor is only a few centimetres higher than the pupil, and his forward view is poor. To exercise proper supervision on takeoff and landing the instructor has a periscope, built into the roof.

Each cockpit has its own canopy, and as in previous MiG trainers these hinge independently under the control of switches in each cockpit. Unlike earlier MiG trainers both canopies hinge upwards, with separate jacks. The seats are downgraded from the KM-1 family used in the single-seaters, and are similar to the early model used in the MiG-21F. This is armed by the closing canopy pressing down on a large hinged arm above the top of the seat. Partly because of this, the canopy over the front (pupil) cockpit has an additional transverse frame in line with the occupant's face, giving the structure greater rigidity. Between the canopies is a substantial fixed portion to which the front canopy is hinged. The rear canopy has a heavier metal centreline frame and metal rear section. The axial central frame incorporates an optical periscope very similar to that fitted to

the MiG-21U family, pulled down from the front by the instructor to raise the upper mirror to the operative position. This upper mirror is normally folded down into a bulged upper fairing above the opaque rear section of the canopy. Unlike fighter rear-view mirrors in the same location, the periscope gives a view ahead of the aircraft. With its aid MiG-23U instructors have landed in extremely bad visibility.

Behind the cockpits the dorsal spine fairing is considerably enlarged, mainly to suit the additional canopy further downstream than in the single-seater. This fairing does not cover additional internal fuel.

Air/air and air/surface missions

Like the avionically downgraded fighters the MiG-23U has the low-power radar, fuselage-mounted pylons (not under the inlet ducts) and the GSh-23L gun. The five inboard stores pylons are normally fitted, twin or triple tandem interface units occasionally being seen. There is no vestige of a rear-fuselage rack, which is reserved for dedicated attack models. At the same time the MiG-23U plays an important role in checking out pupils for air-to-surface missions as well as the more popular air

Above: Only one type of MiG-23U has so far been identified (unlike the profusion of MiG-21 trainer versions). These are on final approach, with instructor periscopes working.

combat, using the gun and (usually) K-13A missiles.

So far all MiG-23U trainers in VVS service seen in the West have had silver-grey external finish, with individual aircraft number painted red or orange. The five stores racks (excluding tank pylons on the outer wings) are fully wired for stores, the right-hand glove pylon being in line with the forward-facing sensor (said to be an ASM guidance aerial) often seen there. Much of the MiG-23U appears like a simplified fighter version, including a long dorsal fin, ILS, high-pressure tyres and SRO-2M IFF above the nose.

One can speculate indefinitely on why the Ministry of Aviation Industry chose to build the MiG-23U with a small radar, when either none or the latest High Lark set would have seemed more cost effective. Most trainers have a peculiarly pronounced tail-down "sit" on the ground, the fuselage attitude varying remarkably with changes in fluid pressure in the main-gear retraction jacks and levered-suspension cylinders. So far as is known, the 23U is not used for initial training in either AAMs or ASMs, but could be used as a front-line combat type in emergency.

43

7
Foreign Operators

THE SOVIET Union is not noted for developing special versions of its warplanes for export, other than downgraded variants from which security-sensitive items of equipment have been eliminated. This is certainly the case with the MiG-23 family, where for almost a decade the exported models were operationally less capable than those of the Soviet VVS.

The initial export fighter, whose true designation is unknown, is called Flogger-E by NATO. It basically comprises the airframe of the original MiG-23MF with the nose of the trainer MiG-23U. This virtually eliminates all-weather interception and stand-off kill capability, though the radar's performance is very much better than nothing (search range 29km, 18 miles, and tracking range 19km, 12 miles). Absence of the big High Lark radar does, however, eliminate use of medium-range radar-guided AAMs such as the R-23R (AA-7 Apex), and the only air-combat

weapons of these fighters are the K-13 family (AA-2 and AA-2-2 Atoll) and the GSh-23L gun. There is no reason why the compact R-60 (AA-8 Aphid) missile should not also be fired.

Having the nose of the trainer also eliminates both the big doppler navigation radar and the infra-red sensor gondola, which further degrades the operational effectiveness of this export variant. This is to a small degree offset by reduced cost, and by the fact that most customers enjoy generally fine weather, making visual interceptions and close-range kills more practical. On the other hand, in this kind of fighting the basic MiG-23 is not in the same class as the F-16 and similar modern air-combat fighters. The Israelis, who have had the opportunity to fly both types, even consider it inferior as a dogfighter to the MiG-21. Certainly the MiG-23's chief test in air combat so far, flown by the Syrian Air Force against Israeli fighters over the Bekaa Valley in 1982, led to a score tentatively put at 82-0, the dominant opposition being almost entirely F-16s. This was perhaps hardly a fair test, because—as has so often been the

Below: Best picture of a non-Warpac MiG-23, this LARAF (Libyan) Flogger-E was seen over the Gulf of Sirte by the US Navy. Missiles are K-13A (AA-2 Atoll) IR-homing weapons.

case in the past—the Soviet-built fighters were flown by rather inexperienced and perhaps disorganized pilots, who had to contend with markedly better fighters flown by outstandingly skilled and aggressive pilots with the enormous extra benefit of overall control from E-2C Hawkeyes.

More advanced export Floggers

Syria is, in fact, one of the fortunate recipients of the much better-equipped MiG-23MF Flogger-G. India has imported Soviet-built MiG-23ML interceptors. Another foreign recipient is the Warsaw Pact member the DDR (German Democratic Republic). Users of the simpler Flogger-E are known to include Afghanistan, Algeria, Cuba, Iraq, North Korea and Libya. Iraq has an extensive combat history with the MiG-23, but surprisingly little tangible information on the Gulf air war has percolated through to the West, and no detailed information on MiG-23 operations. Likewise the Libyan aircraft have probably seen action in several theatres, but again nothing has been published in the Western media.

Surprisingly, the original dedicated attack variant, the MiG-27 Flogger-D, appears never to have been supplied to any user other than the massive initial customer, Frontal Aviation, and to Egypt. Even the upgraded Flogger-J has not been exported except in small numbers—one regiment, about 72 aircraft—to the DDR's Luftstreitkräfte (air force).

In contrast the hybrid MiG-23BN family has been exported quite widely, and apparently without any downgrading other than (one surmises) refusal of the Soviet authorities to export the latest ECM jammer pods and weapons except possibly to members of the Warsaw Pact. Among the latter the air forces of Bulgaria, Czechoslovakia and Poland all operate the BN variant known as Flogger-H, with forward facing target-illuminating blisters added. The slightly earlier Flogger-F has been supplied to the air forces of Afghanistan (it is believed), Algeria, Cuba, Egypt, Ethiopia, Iraq, Lybia, Syria and Vietnam. The total number of BN sub-types exported to these countries is over 500. Egypt also received the

Flogger-E fighter, the Flogger-D attack version and the MiG-23U trainer. In 1974 the Soviet Union supplied a mix of 16 of the single-seaters, plus four trainers, but relations with the superpower deteriorated. Following only about one year of active service at Mersa Matruh air base the whole force was placed in storage, the problems caused by relatively small numbers, and lack of spares and technical support, proving insuperable.

Unofficial exports

In the longer term this was to prove very useful to other interested parties, because most, if not all, of these aircraft were disposed of to governments that would otherwise have found such aircraft very difficult to acquire. At least two were shipped to the People's Republic of China, where they were naturally studied in the minutest detail. Western publications have suggested that a "Chinese copy" might be put into production, even the designation J-11 having been offered for it, but the author knows of no evidence that this is being done. Certainly the Rolls-Royce Spey 200-series would be insufficiently powerful, and the Chinese have no other engine in the required class. Many of the rest of the Egyptian MiG-23s went to the USA, where they joined the clandestine "MiG squadron" based at Groom Lake in the Nellis complex. At the time of writing, no photographs from this source had appeared, nor have the MiGs (which include MiG-21s also) appeared in legitimate Red Flag exercises.

Above: MiG-23BN Flogger-F attack aircraft, seen in a flypast over Cairo in 1974. Briefly based at Mersa Matruh, these aircraft were withdrawn (see text at left) and most are now in the USA. Clearly, a condition of their transfer to that country was that nothing about them should be published.

The workings of state security are often tortuous and hard to comprehend. This is particularly the case when an open society, such as that of the United States, places an absolute clamp on publication of technical details of potentially hostile hardware which the whole world knows to be in its possession. Thus, either the Department of Defense or of State has prohibited publication of design details (except in the most general terms) of the MiG-25 Foxbat, years after an example was dissected and examined in the most minute detail and one of its engines run. In the case of the MiG-23 family, nothing tangible has appeared at all, so that—to his great surprise—the author was able to learn a great deal of unpublished information merely by reading the stencilling on the outer skin of aircraft which had visited the West eight years previously!

He would unquestionably have learned much more from walking around the MiG-27M publicly displayed in India as long ago as October 1984. The amount of information *not* published about the attack versions would fill a book! Not least of the problems is that, as related in the chapter on these aircraft, all MiG-27s have simple fixed inlets and a short afterburner with two-position nozzle, the hybrids with the fighter-type engine installation being designated MiG-23BN. Even today *Jane's* lists the version built under licence in India as the MiG-27M

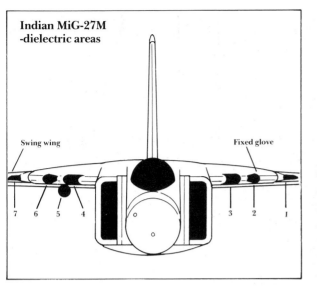

Indian MiG-27M -dielectric areas

Swing wing

Fixed glove

7 6 5 4 3 2 1

Above: Head-on view of the supposed Indian "MiG-27M" showing a comprehensive avionics suite in the leading edge: 1 and 7, EW (probably transmitter) aerials in the dogteeth; 2 and 6, SO-69 RWR aerials; 3 and 4, unknown suppressed leading-edge aerials; 5, underwing pod said to be SAM guidance.

Flogger-J. But back in October 1984 the first of these aircraft to be completed (from kits of parts supplied from Soviet production) was ceremonially rolled out at the Nasik plant of Hindustan Aeronautics. Western commentators appear to have overlooked the fact that it was in all respects a MiG-23BN Flogger-H, with fighter inlets, GSh-23L gun, bomb racks mounted obliquely on the fuselage instead of under the inlet ducts, and a long variable nozzle.

The author infers that, in October 1984, HAL simply had not yet assembled a MiG-27M. The first photograph of the latter emerged in May 1986, and

shows a definitive attack aircraft of the latest type (see overleaf). Not only does it have the simplified engine installation, wing-root extensions and intake-mounted pylons, but under the nose are twin projections which are clearly a previously unknown sensor group. Each resembles a rectangular blade aerial about 9in (230mm) square, but thicker and carrying interesting but unknown details at the tips.

This very important version, of which at least 150 are expected to be produced to equip six IAF squadrons, is being assembled at HAL Nasik using a progressively greater content of HAL-built parts, and it was hoped that by the time MiG-21bis production was completed in 1986 the Indian MiG-27M line would be almost complete licence manufacture, with only a few bought-out components being imported from the Soviet Union. The HAL Koraput factory was by 1986 firmly into licence-production of the Tumanskii R-29-300 engine, again with progressively increasing local content.

So far as is known, no ASMs (air-to-surface missiles) have been exported for use with attack versions of the MiG-23/-27 family, even to air forces within the Warsaw Pact. On the other hand there are many such weapons available on the commercial market, and it is to be expected that in due course the Indian Air Force and other operators will arm these extremely potent attack aircraft with suitable varieties. The same goes for chaff/flare dispensers and ECM jammer pods, which are essential adjuncts to the

Below: Lacking a MiG-27M, Hindustan Aeronautics ceremonially rolled out this MiG-23BN in October 1984. The explanation is given on this page.

पान निषेध्
SMOKING

penetration of defended airspace. The next-generation MiG-29, now also in use with the Indian Air Force, has a comprehensive internal EW (electronic warfare) suite, though it is not yet known if this has been permitted to accompany deliveries to India. The MiG-23 and MiG-27, however, have no such equipment mounted internally, and carriage of an active jammer necessitates occupying a pylon that

Above: The elusive Indian MiG-27M emerged as this book went to press in summer 1986. Stores include (from left) the FAB-500, GP bomb, PTK-250 cluster dispenser, R-60 (Aphid) AAM (made under licence by HAL), S-240 rocket, and four RPK-100 frags.

could otherwise be used for ordnance or tanks. The author believes the usual jammer location in the attack versions is one of the stores pylons on the side of the rear fuselage.

APPENDIX: MiG-23/-27 FLOGGER DATA

DIMENSIONS

Wing span (sweep angle 72°) 26ft 9.5in (8.17m)
    (sweep angle 16°) 46ft 9in (14.25m)
Length (MiG-23MF and U, overall) 59ft 6.6in (18.15m)
    (23BN and 27, overall) 52ft 6in (16.0m)
Height (overall) 14ft 9in (4.5m)
Wing area (gross, 16° sweep) 293.4sq ft (27.26m²)
Taileron (horizontal stabilizer) area 74.06sq ft (6.88m²)
Brake parachute area (fully deployed) 226.0sq ft (21.0m²)

WEIGHTS

	MiG-23MF	MiG-27
Empty	25,940lb (11,766kg)	23,850lb (10,818kg)
Clean gross	36,260lb (16,448kg)	34,170lb (15,500kg)
Maximum takeoff	40,670lb (18,448kg)	44,312lb (20,100kg)

POWERPLANT

One Tumanskii two-spool afterburning turbojet.
MiG-23M and MiG-23U: one R-27 with maximum dry (MIL) rating of 15,430lb (7,000kg) and maximum rating of 22,485lb (10,200kg)
MiG-23MF, MiG-23BN and variants: one R-29B with maximum dry (MIL) rating of 17,635lb (8,000kg) and maximum rating of 27,500lb (12,475kg)
MiG-27 and variants: one R-29-300 with maximum dry (MIL) rating of 17,920lb (8,130kg) and maximum rating of 25,350lb (11,500kg)

PERFORMANCE

MiG-23MF
Maximum speed (clean) at sea level Mach 1.2 (913mph, 1,470km/h); maximum speed (clean, 50 per cent fuel) at high altitude Mach 2.3 (1,520mph, 2,446km/h); service ceiling 61,000ft (18,600m); combat radius (high altitude air-combat mission with four AAMs only) 530 miles (850km), (with centreline drop tank added) 700 miles (1,126km); takeoff and landing ground run (typical) 2,950ft (900m).

MiG-27
Maximum speed (clean) at sea level Mach 0.95 (685mph, 1,102km/h), (clean, 50 per cent fuel) at high altitude Mach 1.6 (1,056mph, 1,700km/h); service 52,500ft (17,000m); combat radius (hi-lo-hi profile with 4,410lb/2,000kg external weapon load and no external fuel) 311 miles (500km), (lo-lo-lo profile) 240 miles (390km); takeoff and landing ground run (clean) 1,800ft (550m), (maximum weight) 4,600ft (1,800m).

PRINTED IN BELGIUM BY
proost
INTERNATIONAL BOOK PRODUCTION